THE NAKED MARKET

THE
NAKED MARKET

Marketing Methods for the 80s

ROBERT HELLER

SIDGWICK & JACKSON
LONDON

To Francesca

First published in Great Britain in 1984
by Sidgwick and Jackson Limited

Copyright © 1984 by Heller Arts

ISBN 0-283-99012-0

Typeset by Tellgate Ltd, London WC2
Printed in Great Britain by
Biddles Ltd, Guildford, Surrey
for Sidgwick and Jackson Limited
1 Tavistock Chambers, Bloomsbury Way
London WC1A 2SG

Contents

Acknowledgements

This book grew out of my association with and writings for *Marketing* magazine, admirably edited by my long-time friend and associate, Tom Lester; I am deeply grateful to him and to his excellent colleagues. I also owe a debt of thanks and enlightenment to the many sources mentioned in the book, notably John Winkler (and his book *Pricing for Results*), John Thackray (the superb US correspondent of *Management Today*) and, among several invaluable publications, the *Financial Times* and the *Harvard Business Review*. I have had kind and efficient assistance from Anne Ferguson and Annabella Gabb: and I owe most special thanks to Anne Leguen de Lacroix for all her unstinting and excellent help. The book would not, of course, have been possible without my many contacts with the men and women who manage the marketing of the companies I've mentioned – and many I have not. It has been a privilege to observe them in the most exciting business times that I (and I expect they) can recall.

Introduction

The years since 1973 have been a marvellous economic decade, believe it or not – even though the oil price explosion did end general rapid Western economic expansion, perhaps for keeps. The marvel was that the same dismal decade saw the creation of more genuine new companies, more new self-made fortunes and more new revolutionary product successes than any such period in history. In the last quarter of the twentieth century world markets have been split wide open, old-line companies have been torn apart, and new-style entrepreneurs have poured through the openings.

Partly, the opportunities have been created by the new technologies which have opened up new industrial avenues, often whole vistas of change and wealth. But even in old markets, where neither micro-circuits, nor genetic engineering, nor any other scientific marvel, has worked any wonders (or ever will), new market opportunities have multiplied. Managers who miss those chances will – and many already have – perished on the shore.

The iron hand of economics, as always, is ruling. The new technologies are breaking through because of plain, clear economic superiority. Take an aged market like cameras (George Eastman invented the Kodak in 1895). Electronics has performed three amazing feats at once – lowering the manufacturing cost of the camera and raising its reliability, while simultaneously and richly enhancing the product's appeal through detailed innovation. That's the key. In a saturated world marketplace, growth in general demand would be slow, in these end-century days, even without world recessions. Marketing used to be that of need: today, it is the marketing of desire.

Create and satisfy a specific, optional desire, and you make vastly more money than somebody who merely meets a real, basic need – in 1982 Apple Computers made a quarter of General Mills' net income though the food giant's sales were 14½ times higher. Specialization, not just that of the dedicated high technology firms like Apple, but also within the old homogeneous markets like bread, is one cause of the greatly enlarged role of genuine marketing expertise in today's successes: but even more important is simple ease of entry. In some of the new boom areas, like personal and other small-scale computing, entry is even simpler than it was for the automobile pioneers before the First World War. As recently as 1976, Apple was started on $1,500. In many fields now, the well-positioned, small specialist can break in before the big market leaders even realize the risk – if, that is, they are asleep at the switch.

The ferocious competition created by differentiated, easy-to-enter and desire-driven markets means that a moment's marketing slumber can easily become the Big Sleep. The market has become naked in many ways; naked, because there's no protection against its forces (even if a government temporarily bails out the feeble, fate always gets them in the end): naked, because changes in management's own world (the job-hopping, the market research explosion, even downright theft) mean that few markets hold any secrets any more – no secrets, that is, which can be kept for long: naked, because most marketplaces are now arenas for naked aggression.

In such a situation, which won't change in this century, success goes to those who combine the highest degree of aggression with the fullest application of intelligence. It's a combination that only the best men and greatest firms manage to keep working effectively down the years. This book shows how these best of marketers succeed, and why: and, just as important, how their victims, time and again, die from wounds which are self-inflicted.

In the years leading up to 2000, every factor that created the extraordinary triumphs of the years from 1973, from the multiplication of markets to the proliferation of technological advance, will become even more intense. The opportunities for the true marketeer who knows his nakedness and dons the right clothes will be still more lucrative. This book is his guide.

SECTION ONE
PRODUCTS

1: The Technological Catch

The more miraculous technology becomes, the more those who manage it require entirely non-technical skills: above all, those of marketing. This essential truth of the Age of Competition was symbolized in unmistakable terms when one John Sculley, a marketing man from Pepsico, was appointed president of Apple: the warmest seat in the hottest high-tech market. In fact, throughout its astonishing growth to a billion dollars of sales in half-a-dozen years, Apple had flourished partly because of what Americans call 'marketing smarts' – but that was in a situation where the gee-whiz company had much of the personal computer market to itself. With that security destroyed, primarily by the invasion of IBM, Apple had no option but to raise its sights several notches: hence Sculley.

Hence, too, the all-or-nothing bet on the Lisa and Macintosh computers, a major advance in technology: but also a step forward in marketing, because the new computers' main attraction – one bound to make sales easier – is that the inexpert can master them in a mere twenty minutes. In other words, high technology is itself a marketing tool, and may well be entirely useless if it isn't geared closely and powerfully to a marketing need that can be economically serviced. (Remember that, by definition, a marketing need that can't be economically serviced might as well not exist).

No more striking proof of this point will ever be provided than the supersonic airliner, Concorde. Forgetting its relatively cramped interior, this is plainly a superior product, delivering its service (air travel) in far more acceptable form: i.e., faster. Real product superiority invariably has the sublime virtue of attracting a premium price. But the premium can't be scaled up indefinitely; it won't necessarily reach a level, either, at which prices will cover the costs of being superior. Believe that it will, and you're liable to end up with a Concorde – a product whose costs are simply too large ever to be matched by the revenue available at any imaginable price.

There's no true marketing pull in such a situation; however desirable the merits of the product, they are never desirable at any price. You can usually tell when irreversible errors of this kind have been committed. The proponents of the mistake produce extraneous arguments to prove that it wasn't a fiasco after all, but a masterstroke of management. Thus Concorde's defenders claimed that the super-jet was a flagship for the conventional flights of British Airways, and that its long and costly genesis had produced spin-offs for the more humdrum products of British industry.

On the first argument, even if £900 million had been a sensible price to pay for a mere flag, there was no evidence, either from BA's financial results for many years or its seat occupancy figures, that the airline had any image advantage over its competitors. Nor does anything confirm the notion that factors which have nothing to do with the actual product or service offered ever help to build sales. Thus the brilliantly cultivated branding of an IBM or a Mercedes-Benz is certainly a most powerful tool: but only in the service of powerful products. Bad IBM products (like its first stab at copiers, or the first version of the PC jr computer) fare like anybody else's. They flop.

As for the second argument, the spin-off one, that is equally feeble. It would make no sense to build a supersonic airliner if you were actually intending to make something else (but what?): it's also quite wrong to pursue the technology-push policy – or, to phrase it another way, the Technological Mousetrap Myth, a delusion which has much British industrial blood on its hands.

This fond belief is that, if you make a better mousetrap, the world will beat a path to your door. The myth is venerable to the point of decrepitude, disproved again and again, and never more comprehensively than by the total defeat of competitors which genuinely had stolen technological marches on IBM in mainframe computers. It didn't matter: IBM was still incomparably stronger in the only place that counts, the marketplace. Yet despite all such evidence, many allegedly marketing-oriented companies still operate on the mousetrap principle; improve the product, they think, and technology push will create the sales.

13

Unfortunately, a few cases exist to encourage managements in this delusion. For example, managers from Michelin, when it achieved wonders of penetration in the tyre market in both Europe and America, had been heard to say that the company had no marketing. According to this interpretation, the French firm merely concentrated on technological superiority and raked in the sales as an invention like its steel-radial tyre inflicted torture on its competitors.

Examine the case more carefully, though, and it's clear that Michelin had plenty of marketing: and excellent marketing, at that. The Michelin tyre man, the guides and so on are only a minor, though valuable, part of the mix. The main thrust down the decades has been to associate Michelin deliberately and consistently with that idea of product superiority. Of course, the product must genuinely be superior: but in its policies on pricing, distribution, advertising and everything else, Michelin preserved the image of premium supplier. The actual technology was part of this marketing package, a weapon used expertly to achieve great force at the point of consumer impact.

The Drugs on the Market

The pharmaceutical companies have long demonstrated the true underlying principle. It isn't just a question of developing a new and more powerful or efficacious drug. That is the first name of the game: but the second name is marketing – achieving the maximum impact on the medical profession in the minimum time, and in the sure knowledge that, sooner rather than later, powerful competition will arrive on the scene. What the drug companies have experienced ever since chemotherapy got into its wonderful post-war stride is now common to most industries: a desperate competitive scramble to catch up (and if possible, overtake) whenever a genuine innovation appears on the market.

In some cases, the competition will take desperate measures even before it has a weapon in hand. When SmithKline launched its anti-ulcer drug, Tagamet, on the West German market, it found its guns had been temporarily spiked. A competitor had rushed out a heavy advertising campaign which conveyed the impression that its modified existing product was the wonder-drug for which German doctors and their patients had been waiting. It took great effort, much money and also much time before SK recovered from a weak German

14

start with one of the strongest products the industry has ever seen.

This single wonder-drug (British-developed, incidentally) has transformed the Philadelphia company into a wonder-company. Over the decade to 1983, its earnings per share rose by 20.8 per cent annually, while its deliriously happy investors reaped a total reward of 19.7 per cent compound. The ulcer relief which Tagamet provides spun so much money (SK's 15.5 per cent net return on sales was second highest of the top 500 US companies) that it underpinned a largely new, immensely successful world-wide marketing operation.

So far, so very wonderful. But such success carries within it the seeds of severe problems. Essentially, it's no different from one of the oldest strategic conundrums: the one-product poser. When a company is riding a commercial Mill Reef or Eclipse, the magical horse that wins all the prizes, it's hard to think of the horse being shot from under you. A Volkswagen management riding the Beetle, or a BSR board booming on record-changers, is inherently unlikely to prepare for the evil day – a calamity in which the managers simply don't believe, but which, as in both the above cases, is certain to arrive.

VW even compounded its error, proving that lightning can strike you down twice in the same place, by letting its Golf model (known as the Rabbit in the US) run too long in a world market sector where it was, year by year, attacked by newer models – from Japan as well as Europe. As a result, VW sales in the US, where it was once the fourth largest selling marque after Chevrolet, Ford and Plymouth, collapsed to a tenth of their peak level.

But drug companies are wiser. They know that, even if competition and lapsed patients don't, one day, make the eggs less golden, sudden disaster can always turn a dream product into a nightmare. It happened to Fisons before its Proxicromil drug had even reached the market. As soon as grave safety doubts surfaced, Fisons was left with no room to manoeuvre: the curtain had to be rung down, no matter what the cost. The same no-option decision faced Eli Lilly when deaths were shown to result after treatment by an existing anti-arthritis drug, Opren.

The company, during an appalling run of bad publicity, put off its evil day as long as possible – which proved to be far too long. But it's not hard to see how reluctant any marketer must be to stop a smash hit in its tracks. Only consider the plight of SmithKline, whose drug marketers were confronted, not with the type of hard and ineluctable

15

facts that torpedoed Proxicromil and Opren, but at one point with a scare – raised by some medical experts – that their beloved Tagamet might carry a risk of cancer: and at a time when other medical opinion was swinging towards the newly arrived Zantac from Glaxo.

The marketers in such a situation are damned if they do endorse the critical view, because they will surely lose sales enormously: they may be damned if they don't – if the critics prove right. In fact, the natural human tendency is for management to rally to the cause, to blot out the hostile evidence and to emphasize, even exaggerate, one's own case. But in the end the truth will out. Nothing will avert crisis if a company like Fisons or Eli Lilly truly has drawn the black spot.

The Wonder-Portfolio

The wonder-company that relies on one technological wonder-product, no matter how superb, is on fundamentally unsafe ground. The best consumer marketers have long known that safety lies, not in products, but in portfolios of products. That defence was what enabled Procter & Gamble to ride through the withdrawal, again on grounds of medical danger, of its Rely tampons: or Johnson & Johnson to survive with remarkable ease the dreadful disaster of having to withdraw and then relaunch its Tylenol capsules after some maniac or maniacs unknown had poisoned some of the supply.

Note that the idea isn't to diversify for its own sake. The point is rather that successful exploitation of the wonder-product necessarily involves, as noted, the development of many corporate strengths other than the technology itself. The brilliant marketing company exploits both the technology and these essential strengths: in marketing, these always include (or should) branding and distribution. Thus Canon has very sensibly sold all its non-photographic developments under the brand it has so deliberately built up in cameras: the success of the copiers reinforces that of the cameras and vice versa – while it also happens to be true that the image technology built up in cameras has direct relevance to copying.

In contrast, Konishiroku, one of Canon's rivals in the field, sold its film under the Sakura brand name, its cameras under the Konica banner, its plain paper copiers as U–Bix and absolutely nothing under the name of the company itself. However excellent its technology (and Konishiroku has many innovations to its credit), that policy tied a hand behind the company's back in all three markets and helped to explain why, despite huge sales of film, in which Canon does not compete, the firm is less than half Canon's size. Significantly, in 1983 the Sakura film brand name was changed – to Konica.

The portfolio principle rests on the certainty that channels of distribution, communication and very often production can carry more than one vessel along them. The wise company, high-tech or low, adds to that knowledge the equal certainty that, since competition will always overtake an innovation, the first public appearance of the latter must always be seen, within the company, as the prelude to the next innovation – the development which will always give the company's portfolio its market edge.

Sony knew when the Walkman personal cassette player appeared that it only had six months before competition arrived: so the first enhancement of the Walkman had to be completely ready by the time of the original launch. Any honeypot will attract other, maybe bigger, bears. That is one risk of being best which nobody can avoid. But not being best carries even greater risks. The best companies have mastered the trick of minimizing the dangers that technological triumph may be transient by the non-technical management and marketing successes which, in contrast, last for a corporate lifetime – and may make that life, for all practical purposes, everlasting.

2: Why Marketing Needs Management

The marketing on which a company like Apple is now forced to depend differs in kind, scope and power from that which reigned in the better-protected markets of the post-war seller's paradise. One critical difference is that marketing is now seen in proper perspective: neither as an add-on to boost the corporate selling power, nor as a wonderful new discipline about to swamp the entire company, sweeping all before it. Today's marketing is indeed company-wide; but it's an integrating, animating force that binds together the other functions – and doesn't subjugate them.

The relationship can be seen clearly from what happened at Vauxhall Motors when Australian John Bagshaw was brought in as marketing director: Bagshaw found that vitally important fleet orders had been lost by failure to meet delivery promises. He went back to the production people – who improved their performance so sharply that Bagshaw could keep his promises to the letter. That helped greatly to propel the company's market share from 8 to 12 per cent (now 17.7 per cent) and to push Bagshaw into responsibility for production and on to still higher things in General Motors.

The connection between manufacturing performance and marketing capability is too obvious to be ignored: although that doesn't stop people from ignoring it. Delivery and quality are the two touchstones. The saving grace for management is that the revolution in production technology and methods (as the Japanese have shown) has made it much easier to reach and maintain proper standards. Without that improvement, for instance, Sir Clive Sinclair would never have been able to do it again: or rather, do it for the first time. His brilliant pioneering thrust into the calculator market foundered on

18

quality problems so awful that they have passed into industrial legend.

The misadventure proved that even a man like Sinclair, with innovative prowess of almost Mozartian proportions, needs more, much more. Getting the goods to the market isn't enough: having them lapped up by the paying customers isn't enough, either. Administrative and productive capacity has to match inventive brilliance if a calculator-style come-uppance is to be avoided.

In fact, Sinclair's past record in such matters gave no hint that he could achieve such prodigies with a low-cost computer, which, in no time at all, overtook the Pets and Tandys in the US market. The comparison needs to be qualified by the fact that Sinclair's machine was much cheaper. But that, too, is a tribute to the maestro, who correctly saw that a little computer then costing just under $200 (by a single buck) would be irresistible to Americans – even though it couldn't actually do much in the way of serious computing.

In fact, the same kind of quality allegations were levelled at the ZX80 and ZX81 as at the original Sinclair calculators. The creator, though, could afford to be adamant that the quality faults, this time, had been eliminated. The very same integrated circuitry that enabled Sinclair to bring out the machines so cheaply also vastly reduced the room for sloppy production. Technology couldn't, alas, resolve the administrative problems (like getting through to the company on the phone, or achieving enough output to meet demand) which persisted into Sinclair's computer era. Such faults are par for the course of a man who cheerfully admits that he has no great interest in management. The perpetual risk is that his Achilles heel will again prove fatal: in marketing, the fundamental principle is that business is an indivisible whole.

Before Sinclair's calculator breakthrough aborted, one marketing consultant sought to argue that the inventor had disproved the above tenet: by splitting manufacture from marketing, sub-contracting all production to suppliers, Sinclair, so this expert said, had made a world-shattering business breakthrough as well. Who needed manufacture? The answer, as events showed, is that marketers do. Sub-contracting only worked so well for Sinclair the second time round because of the change in technology and because he used a single, much more powerful supplier – Timex.

The initial success in the States belonged to Timex as much as to Sinclair, whose machine carried its manufacturer's name in the US.

19

Without that marketing (and manufacturing) power, it is doubtful whether Sinclair could have survived the onslaught of the ambitious American competitors alerted by his very successes to the new growth market. They promptly started to leave no stone unturned as they strove to steal Sinclair's clothes. Nowhere has there been a more convincing demonstration of the speed with which today's naked markets change and weaken.

A scant two years after Sinclair had so surprisingly cracked the US market, Timex was caught in a ferocious price war. The $199 tag became a fond memory; even the 1982 level of $99.95 melted away to $29.97, then to $15, in a market where two far more powerful competitors (Texas Instruments and Atari) had already been forced into loss. In this situation, with sales plummeting despite the price cuts and TI's withdrawal from the market, Sinclair was probably lucky not to have built the integrated, managed organizational machine that meeting the challenge demands: lucky because that corporate machine, with its inevitable overheads, might well have failed – just like Timex, forced to withdraw from US home computers in its turn.

Polaroid's Instant Error

The degree of that corporate risk is shown by the strange events at Polaroid. This great innovative multi-national, famous for its marketing and its technology alike, suffered declines in sales for four consecutive years. Companies with billion-dollar turnovers in markets that are still growing hardly ever lose sales in a single year, let alone four. Polaroid's experience showed that management mistakes can undermine even a classic position of marketing strength. But in naked markets what used to take many years has been speeded up, like slapstick chases in Mack Sennett movies: the timespan of destruction has been telescoped.

It isn't simply that Polaroid was too much of a one-product company – although that's the diagnosis proffered by its own chief executive, William J. McCune, Jr, successor to the legendary Edwin Land. The fact that McCune was in his mid-sixties when Land left the scene drops a strong hint: the great businessman/inventor had stayed on too long – and by leaving a veteran of his own regime in charge Land stacked the odds heavily against the company striking out in any new directions, let alone the right ones.

McCune saw Polaroid's problem as over-dependence on instant photography: *ergo*, it had to diversify into non-camera, non-consumer markets. It's an old, sad story. A company whose basic business is faltering blames the trouble, not on mismanagement of the base activity which it knows and loves, but on lack of new markets it knows nothing about. Yet Polaroid's critical threat is basic: the coming of competition in instant photography has coincided with a fall in instant's market share – largely because orthodox camera firms have been breathtakingly innovative: what with endless single-lens reflexes, compacts and now discs and videos, Polaroid has been attacked from all sides.

To make matters worse, conventional colour film has been improved to startling degrees, with same-day processing on tap – while the filmless camera is on the horizon as yet another threat. The competitive catalogue shows that Polaroid committed the classic error immortalized by that great guru of marketing, Professor Ted Levitt: it saw itself in the business of *instant* photography – not of photography, whatever its nature. The narrow-front strategy had kept it well away from the powerful Eastman Kodak for the years of supergrowth. But eventually expansion and product maturity always demand a switch to a broader concept. The main broadening at Polaroid was to make its own film – previously contracted out to Kodak. That only precipitated the Goliath's competition in instant cameras: and Land and McCune's diversifications, which only generated a third of sales in 1982, could give little protection against that.

Fully exposed, Polaroid's picture plainly needed merger and/or partnership as the right strategic choice. Having roused the not-so-sleeping Kodak giant, Polaroid should surely have gone the whole way – buying into conventional film and cameras. There were, after all, plenty of possible partners – not only Japanese, but German and even American (3M, for one, has been striving to break Kodak's stranglehold on film). Products like Polaroid's computer-linked printers, whatever their commercial virtues, are no answer to a problem of such strategic magnitude. As one Polaroid executive said to *Business Week*, 'You can't stay on this path and assume it's going to be O.K.' In the naked market, no position is secure – even Kodak has only avoided Polaroid's trap by means of a phenomenal pace of innovation in the 1970s and 1980s: and even that didn't save it from a heavy fall in profits as Japanese competition bit deeply into margins.

Polaroid has been innovative all its life, as noted, and has by no means slackened its own pace. But the photographic innovations have all been instant (including the ill-fated instant home movie venture, Land's last fling, which coincided fatally with the coming of video). The tragedy is that the management which had been powerful enough to carry Polaroid through the growth era of instant photography proved inadequate to meet the challenge of a market where instant was no longer enough.

The Bad Paradox of Good Design

By what seems a curious paradox, the actual design of Polaroid's products, cumbersome and unlovely in the years of supergrowth, became elegant and brilliant in the period of mounting problems. The paradox disappears when a few more examples of the same phenomenon are noted – such as those contained in a report in the *Financial Times* just before the 1981 Car of the Year was about to be named. The reporter noted that Rover (the 3500), Porsche (the 928) and Lancia (the Delta) had all won the prize in previous years, but had received no prizes in the marketplace. 'Yet cars that were voted into second place – the Ford Fiesta and Opel Kadett, to name but two – have sold like hot cakes.'

The observation should give the marketing-minded food for some fairly furious thought, and not just about cars. It's the same thought that occurred to a company chairman contemplating a faulty electric razor: he grumbled, fairly or unfairly, that companies with an immaculate reputation for aesthetic and exemplary design, such as Braun, Bang & Olufsen and Olivetti, never produced contents whose performance matched the beauty of the package.

The proposition is not likely to appeal to the managements concerned. But it is true that, if you ask hi-fi buffs about Bang & Olufsen, you observe a distinct curl of the lip. And it's also true that the bestselling Lettera 22, a world-famous design, was heavy and not particularly pleasant to operate. Unlike Bang & Olufsen, Olivetti was not appealing to a well-heeled, upper-crust market to which appearance mattered more than function. The Olivetti range was for the general public – and the typewriter's weaknesses in this respect, in hindsight, look symptomatic of the failings that once almost bankrupted the great Italian company.

The distinction between form and function neatly illustrates why marketing needs management. It explains why, even though the winners of the Car of the Year award both gain and exploit the prize's considerable publicity value in the market-place, the better-managed runners-up win the glittering commercial prizes. Critics who make awards and write about design are inevitably most impressed by form, while motoring journalists (who judge this particular prize) are by definition enthusiasts, people who don't approach a set of wheels with the same attitudes as the family motorist.

The manager is in neither position – not if he is doing his duty by his market and his customer. The true hot-cake cars are designed with the functional market requirement as the starting point: the contents in a sense determine the package. A result which is still good enough to earn second place from the professionals must be a highly successful compromise – with the dimensions of compromise determined mostly by trade-offs between cost and price.

Give the designer his head, however, and his natural response will be to place the package first and foremost. As noted in contrasting Bang & Olufsen and Olivetti, the manager may have good reason to go along with this policy. If he is aiming to sell expensive hi-fi to the average pair of ears, or costly luggage to an expensive pair of hands, that makes magnificent sense: the visual excellence, like the high price, reassures the purchaser that he's buying top functional quality as well – even if he isn't.

The rationale, though, is exactly the same as that which produced the Ford Fiesta. The design must suit the marketing purposes of the product. A high-design, low-function strategy, though, carries higher risks than a low-design, high-function one. That's because the former implies a high price, which leaves plenty of room, in cost terms, for a competitor to attack, tempting the top of the market with quality that goes more than skin-deep.

Not only that: the high-design company also faces a rude awakening if the performance doesn't match the package and the promise. That has happened with the three prizewinning cars mentioned above. For the Rover 3500, the Porsche 928 and the Lancia Delta, a miss was even worse than a mile. In the demanding, capricious naked market of today, it's not the applause of the critics but the roar of the crowd which has to be earned. This isn't to say that managers and marketers should ignore design. Far from it – refusal by management to admit design into the important processes of the firm is pernicious in the extreme.

23

The truth is that there can't be design, good or bad, without management – even if it is only management by abdication. The decision to do nothing about design, or to let a bad design run, is a decision about design, and a rotten one. Good design includes performance, technology, image, cost, manufacturing method and development potential. Thus, whatever aspect management wears, design is included in it or includes it. Unfortunately, the tendency has been for both management and the design world to think of design almost as aesthetics, as something added on – hence the chairman's wife syndrome, in which an important corporate design decision is relegated to the status of choosing chintz curtains.

This disregard for design systems is a luxury which cannot be afforded in the new Age of Competition in which, even if growth gets faster, the affluent societies of the West, saturated with consumer and industrial goods, will be dominated by a trend which has become ineluctable: the great switch to specialized, smart, differentiated markets. In satisfying the markets of desire, rather than those of need, design must be paramount.

Thus, in world markets, the hallmark of the Japanese approach has been constant, with continuous upgrading of rival designs. The pace of Japanese innovations is so bewildering by Western standards that it tends to obscure the great cleverness with which the novelties are packaged. Even in cars, where Japanese products still don't rank in the forefront of design, the offerings are being continually improved. For a long time, too, the Japanese car has met the basic requirement of any design: to give the consumer a perceived high value for money.

That is good management and true marketing: the task is to direct the efforts of the design team towards areas where high pay-off can be achieved – and then management must see that it *is* achieved. A perfectly designed product that doesn't sell is a contradiction in terms. In this age, the designer's income and the manager's alike depend on maintaining a flow of highly marketable and profitable products. The work of the designer has a vital contribution to make to both parts of the equation: the marketability and the profits. The alleged dualism or dichotomy between management and design is thus as totally false as that between sales and production. Either they all go hand in hand or, in the Age of Competition, none will go at all. Production is sales is design is marketing: and they all add up to, and need, management.

3: The Market Hits That Flop

It's not only a marvellous design (marvellous, that is, in the eyes of the designer and possibly the beholder) that can flop. The same awful fate can overtake a magnificent market hit: that is, a product which achieves maximum recognition in the marketplace, enormous word-of-mouth advertising (the best and cheapest kind) and a high level of consumer desirability. These are among the characteristics of a superbly successful launch: but, as every launcher knows, that isn't even half the battle.

Few initial marketing operations, for instance, have ever been handled with such impressive skill, such remarkable *éclat*, as the launch of the De Lorean car. The same question is raised by the cases of con-men down the ages; why didn't John Z. De Lorean concentrate where he was brilliant (promotion and publicity) and make millions thereby, instead of losing a fortune by doing what he was bad at – making and selling a marketable product?

The invariable answer is that the same faults of character that generate the public impact impel their possessor towards deception. The De Loreans of this world represent in extreme form an archetypal marketing menace; the fizzing fellow with the flamboyant manner and techniques, who operates to immense public effect, but whose ultimate impression on the public (in the only terms that count, those of sales and profits) falls far short of the image – or, as De Lorean called it, 'the Dream'.

The dreamer's professional weaknesses were evident long before he and his gull-wing car came to grief in one of the strangest business sagas of the late twentieth century. The weakness was evident from a glance at a typical De Lorean ad in the *New Yorker*. Risks shriek out from the purple prose. 'Your eyes skim the sleek, sensuous steel body, and all your senses tell you "I've got to have it". . . . It all began with one man's vision of the perfect personal luxury car. . . . Of course, everyone stares as you drive by. . . . After all, you're the one Living the Dream.'

Clearly, the One Man (whose visionary face stuck out from under the gull-wing doors in the ad) was living, or at any rate advertising, in a bygone Detroit age: the one in which he grew up, and whose death left even his former employer, General Motors, struggling to get on technical and financial terms with the new era. In a day when function rather than form dominated consumer choice; miles per gallon outweighed dreams of glory; and keeping up with, or ahead of, the Joneses was less enrapturing than it used to be, De Lorean and his dream were obsolete.

But putting that aside, the De Lorean case is a perfect example. because of its fraudulence and exaggerations, of the dangers which dog new projects. All of them contain an element of dream, the necessary enthusiasm which explains such unnecessary phenomena as over–optimistic interpretation of initial sales data. Early sales, hyped up by the sheer pressure of the launch, are very often misleading. Quite possibly, those tales of De Lorean's dream-car selling like hot cookies and fetching a colossal premium may even have been true: they told absolutely nothing about the real impact of the car in the market. It takes a long time and careful analysis before confident assessments of underlying demand can be made and secure increases in production authorized.

It wasn't surprising that half the cars ever made in Belfast ended up in stock. To anyone who protests that you can't draw any lessons from a character like De Lorean (who used to sport a T-shirt that lit up with the words 'I am a con-man'), or from a project backed by a foolish government with taxpayers' money, the answer is that many an honest marketer and many a decent corporate backer have ended up in exactly the same hole.

Enthusiasm is a prerequisite of successful marketing, and enthusiasm is difficult to contain within bounds – especially if the management desperately needs the project, as did the Northern Ireland government. Those who desperately want something to come true soon start to believe that it is true; and the very marketing razzmatazz that is supposed to seduce the public seduces the backers.

26

Often, the seduction is so powerful that the executives concerned lock themselves into a most painful position; damned to huge losses if they cut off the pet project; probably damned to even bigger ones if it carries on.

Yet marketing analysis should have shown De Lorean's backers that the Dream was doomed, long before they threw out the baby and the bathwater. One of the oldest and soundest adages in advertising is that the product must match the promise. Exactly the same must be true of the rest of the marketing process. The De Lorean car lacked the distribution, quality, cost structure, marketing universe, engineering, etc. that were required to make any kind of reality out of the Dream. Against those deficiencies, a spectacularly high level of market recognition can make little difference.

The Three-Runner Rule

It's not only the phoney marketing hit, however, that can lose money by the million. So can a product that is a genuine, long-run marketing success. That sounds like a contradiction in terms – but anyone who thinks the paradox hard to resolve should consider the case of the *Sunday Times*, before it dropped into the lap of Rupert Murdoch. What must have attracted the Australian was the Sunday paper's supremacy in one of Britain's best marketplaces. Its strength among the big spenders, major decision-takers, fashionable taste-leaders and all other financially desirable fauna is beyond challenge – thanks to no mean feat to repositioning.

The product's mastery was made possible by progressing from the stodgy, old Kemsley days (when the paper once, briefly, lost its circulation lead to the *Observer*) to the modern, thrusting, trend-setting paper of today: but without weaking its half-Nelson hold on its traditional, more conservative readership. The same Thomson management, however, showed how difficult it is to straddle a market by the now notorious error of trying to move *The Times* simultaneously up-market (aiming at the specialized readership of the *Financial Times*) and down-market (hoping to pick off the far larger readership of the *Daily Telegraph*). Since each target was unattainable, let alone both, *The Times* inevitably plunged into its long series of large losses: and there, in 1980, it found a sister-in-sorrow: none other than the superbly placed *Sunday Times*.

Having by and large got its marketing beautifully right, the Sunday paper ran into losses of £4 million. The usual answer to such a paradox is that the King of the Jungle is prowling in a market where nobody can find a feed. Up to a point, this is true. National newspapers have been fighting to preserve their prosperity ever since television went commercial – but this can't have been a major factor for the *Sunday Times,* which, like Heineken's beer, refreshes the parts other media cannot reach: even in the long Thatcher recession, its market should have stayed reasonably buoyant.

There is, however, a more important point: the overcrowding of Sundays. Heller's Rule of Markets states that most markets can only support a leader, a runner-up and one specialist. With more, everybody may suffer – even the Number One. However, the *Sunday Times* had a lead over its too-many competitors that was so unassailable and so clearly recognized by the market that its profits, while made consistently enough (in seventeen of the twenty years to 1980), should certainly have been better. Apologists will argue that the brute power of the British printing unions is entirely to blame. But that grotesque situation, with some men actually paid large sums for not working, and others paid far too much for far too little, is only the worst, the most reprehensible, example of a general syndrome. The *Sunday Times* simply spent excessively and didn't pause to count the costs.

True, the outpouring of cash went in part to maintain product and market dominance. But a basic principle always applies. All expenditure must generate an adequate return. In other words, get the most for the least: it's no trick to get the most from the most, as Hoover found in the days of its door-to-door army of sales engineers. In marketing terms, the results were fantastic: but so was the cost. And the *Sunday Times* duly paid the inevitable penalty.

The overcrowding effect isn't inevitable for the Number One, anyway. The mainframe computer market was a perfect illustration of the Three-Runner Rule: IBM first, Honeywell second and the rest nowhere, with the specialist role (either in very large and powerful machines or, at the opposite extreme, small to tiny ones) filled at different times and in different circumstances by companies like Control Data, Amdahl, DEC and Apple.

But IBM maintained both its supremacy and its profitability by concentrated marketing management which, even when it missed an opportunity, never lacked the resources to remedy its error – however colossal. By never relaxing its grip, IBM made its main-line, mainframe competitors pay the entire price of overcrowding. They incurred huge, heavy losses: even though, for a period of several years, the anti-trust action brought by the US Justice Department inhibited some, maybe a great deal, of the natural vigour that IBM would otherwise have shown.

Anti-trust considerations certainly played a role in another American illustration that the price of profitable leadership is eternal vigilance. For decades, the US car market perfectly illustrated Heller's Rule: General Motors was first (by miles); Ford, second (but also profitable); Chrysler, third and hopeless; American Motors was only viable in a profitable specialist niche (compact cars for a while, Jeeps at all times). But the pattern was shattered by the rise of the import tide. Only import quotas on Japanese cars stopped them driving Chrysler (even after the company's celebrated recovery) and possibly even Ford to the wall.

And what was GM doing all this time? The years of restraining its domestic market ambitions because of anti-trust fears saw GM's labour costs rise far above non-US competition, its productive efficiency drop far below, its models become uncompetitive, and its innovative ability became stunted. The result, when recession coincided with incompetence, was a massive earnings collapse to a mere ½ per cent of sales in 1981 – made by a company with a dominant market share. Yet as GM promptly showed by its massive $50 billion comeback drive, the resources required to defend profitable leadership were there all the time. They were simply not properly deployed. When they were, Number One went right back on top.

The Markets of Death

There are, however, some markets which support far more than three richly profitable entrants. They aren't in heaven, but in the suspended hell of warfare. When the hellishness becomes real, as in Vietnam or the Falklands, the market test for military procurement is never the price tag, the bang per buck, but the effectiveness of the bang. In the aftermath of actual conflict, in fact, spending is liable to get a boost, not only from replacement, but from remedy of any ineffectiveness laid bare.

True, there have been times, as under President Carter in the US or Labour in Britain, when cutbacks in defence spending for budgetary reasons have created some havoc among the marketers of death. But in both countries, new governments dedicated to defence hastened to raise the ante: the Reagan bounty, for example, added up to a 12 per cent annual boost in spending as far as the eye could see, or the missile could fly. So why aren't the recipients of these riches, the makers of these market hits, the rulers of the economy?

The explanation is the same as that for another phenomenon: that the world growth stakes have been led not by the high-defence spending superpowers, the US and the USSR, but by the defence niggards – like Japan and West Germany. At the level of the firm, as of the nation, military business in general leads nowhere, except to more military business. There have, true, been some spectacular spin-offs from defence billions in the United States – notably the original impetus to the silicon chip. But who landed the largest bonanzas? Not the defence moguls; the big winners have been people, like the Apple personal computer king Steven Jobs, who were barely born when the Apollo programme blasted off.

By the same token, as noted in Chapter 1, if the technological spin-off exists that was originally supposed to justify the ruinous expense of Concorde, that cornucopia is remarkably well concealed. The truth is that developing essentially one-off items, priced on a cost-plus basis, for the military or the government bears no useful relationship to making multi-copy models for the masses – which is where the world markets lie. It may well be that the wonders created in the military zone have miraculous application in ordinary life. But effectively the transfer is no easier than translating any scientific or technological breakthrough into an economic one.

Certainly, the process is not facilitated by the fact that the markets of death are, on the whole, far more profitable than those of peace – with the vast added advantage in cash flow terms that the military customer pays up front, and thereafter on some basis that usually adds up to cost-plus. Civilian markets offer few such parallels, which is why the habits encouraged by dealing with military customers cut so little ice in civilian commerce.

The moral is exactly the same as with the *Sunday Times* and even the De Lorean Dream. The true measure of marketing success isn't public impact and awareness; it isn't the established strength and superiority of the product and its market position; it isn't the ability to serve a customer who doesn't have to count the cost with his heart's desire. The true test is providing people who have the option to refuse your offer with a product or service which they want to buy at a price which they can afford and which offers a large margin over cost: large enough to finance the investment and improvement which will undoubtedly be required. It's a sad reflection that the British economy would be far better off if, instead of building Concorde, the country had given birth (as its French supersonic partners did) to Baron Marcel Bich. His products? The cheap ball-point pen and the throwaway razor.

4: From Product to Commodity

When is a product not a product? When it's a commodity, of course. Once upon a time, in most markets, the best product was the one that everybody needed – nuts and bolts, say, or fertilizers and textiles. So greatly have market conditions changed that today the fate which all companies should fear starts when a product does become a commodity – meaning (as above) that everybody uses it; but also that too many people sell it, so that prices are held down, and nobody earns much from an offering which accounts for too much turnover to be easily abandoned.

Nuts and bolts and fertilizers have long since crossed the dividing line between product and commodity – though where that great divide comes exactly is difficult to say. Like being in love, it's a situation you recognize at once when it arrives; or perhaps the condition is more like falling out of love. For the achievement of commodity status is a terrible let-down. The beloved product, with a price that could be managed and massaged, and with profits that rose as the learning curve worked its magic, reducing costs as cumulative production increased, suddenly becomes, at the worst, a licence to lose money: at the best, a cash cow, to be milked as long as there's anything in the udder.

More often than not, the great divide is crossed because of over-capacity, sometimes created by a fall in demand, but also frequently the result of the Rubber Type Market. Rubber type is what journalists wish they had when a favourite headline fails to fit the allotted space. The Rubber Type Market is identified by the fact that, when all the market shares of all the producers, as reported by the said producers, are added together, they come to considerably more than 100 per cent.

Extrapolate this endearing tendency into the future, and you can easily arrive at 200 per cent – and that may, alas, turn out to be 100 per cent more than actual demand.

The Japanese seem particularly vulnerable to this species of mathematical illusion. First in shipbuilding, then in steel (to name but two industries), they persisted in building huge increments in capacity without apparently working out where the production might be marketed. The same process appears to have been at work in cars. In 1983, world surplus capacity in cars was something like 40 per cent: yet the Japanese, even while their emissaries were promising to take it easy on complaining competitors in Britain and West Germany, were putting in manufacturing capacity for another 3 million.

The truth may be that, because of the rise in oil prices, the congestion on the roads, the slowdown in world growth and some element of sheer saturation, the motor industry has its glory days behind it, in any case – although in the heady sales days of 1983–4, nobody believed so. Impinge on this condition with huge increments in capacity, and it's clear what the result must be: the Commodity Car. In so complicated a market, it won't be as simple as that, of course. Specialists like Daimler Benz and BMW, with production capacities of under half a million, should be relatively secure. But the huge producers, like Ford and General Motors, have already been forced into a position where, if they had to match true Japanese prices, based on costs lower by $1,500 to $2,000 a car, the car would be a commodity with several vengeances.

The Truth About Textiles

As in cars, the normal reaction of threatened producers in these circumstances is to seek protection (by import quotas, voluntary or otherwise) while rationalizing and modernizing for all they are worth (a worth which, in the case of GM, adds up to almost double all the other US car firms put together). But generally the counteraction only puts off the evil day. The force that turns products into commodities is that of harshly applied economics. That's why few industries, even in an economically blighted Britain, have suffered the same number of false dawns and cruel awakenings as textiles. The merging of Carrington Viyella into Vantona in 1983 only marked one more stage in a journey, so far almost entirely downhill, which began with the

33

1960s' decision of two industrial giants, ICI and Courtaulds, that they could save the textile day, even in the face of the tide of imported commodities.

Their efforts were far from co-ordinated – not surprisingly, since Giant A had attempted, to its great discomfiture, to grab an unwilling Giant B. They set off along different tracks for the same destination: at Courtaulds, Lord Kearton bought up and absorbed the end–users of fibres, the textile manufacturers; at ICI, the board pumped money into its chosen vessels, independent customers for its products, only to see most founder, taking down with them large, drowning chunks of chemical capital.

The ghastly calamities which befell ICI clients like Klinger, Carrington & Dewhurst, etc., were to some extent self-inflicted. However hard they tried, few textile men ever got their marketing right. Only one of ICI's protégés (although the protection proved evanescent) had a superlative sense of where the market was heading: the wayward wizard of Viyella, Joe Hyman. Almost his last big decision, before his board dramatically dumped him, was to invest heavily in polyester-cotton – even though some of the biggest downstream customers (including the mighty Marks & Spencer) didn't agree that these were the fabrics of the future.

Whether even Hyman's genius could have coped with the vicissitudes of the 1970s is a second open question. What's certain is that the economic forces which produced the textile takeovers in the first place were inexorable. Maybe the two sponsoring giants, over-influenced by their own huge over-investments in basic fibres, had never got close enough to the market, anyway, despite their costly downstream stakes. In any event, efforts to buck the commodity trend (notably Courtaulds' doomed new Lancashire cotton textile plants) were futile.

The only road to truly profitable survival led up-market, as Dawson International has shown most spectacularly. Vantona and Tootal, for instance, had vast rises in turnover (fivefold and more than double, respectively, in a decade) during years in which their profitability slumped by as much as half from the peaks. That measures the extent to which import-led competition has maintained enormous market pressures – and raises an open question. Would the textile manufacturers have made a better fist of relative failure if the Big Daddies had stayed clear all along?

There's some evidence to show that this would – or at least could – have happened. Without a lifeboat, companies are forced either to sink or swim. You can see the process at work most spectacularly in Japan, with its proliferation of competitors in industry after industry. In that economy the weak sisters refuse to die, or aren't allowed to by large parents: so they are likely to launch huge efforts, either to make the business work by major upheaval, or to engage and succeed in alternative activities: especially since (because of the lifetime employment practice) there is no job market for redundant executives. Such efforts can produce more formidable competition still.

Divestment v. Diversification

It's not generally open in Japan to take the obvious course which is the last, but perhaps the best, resort – divestment. Witness the fertilizer company, Fisons, which plunged into ambitious corporate planning. It ended up with huge over-capacity and tiny profits. That judgement was written in my book, *The Naked Manager*, a decade ago, but the second sentence applied to its subject just as severely as the 1980s began. From one angle, the sale in 1982 of the fertilizer business, the company's heartland, shows how hard it can be to retrieve false steps. From another angle, the subsequent success shows that the sale of heartland businesses (especially for a badly needed £50 million) may be absolutely right. Without selling, indeed, it may be desperately difficult to escape from the faltering heartbeat.

These obsolete businesses remain obstinately large. Despite the undoubted hit of its Intal anti-asthma drug, Fisons still had fertilizer sales that were twice as large as any other division's in 1980. There is a standard, classic strategy for dealing with such outsize problems: *reculer pour mieux sauter* – cutting back to a core of efficient and efficiently manned plants, and then concentrating on accurately aimed marketing to exploit strengths and minimize weaknesses.

The strategy seldom results in a viable and truly profitable business, however. For Fisons, nothing could change the fact that fertilizers had been a murderous market for years, with ICI calling the tune both by its economic power (with twice Fisons' volume) and its marketing habits (competing with everybody, even the small local suppliers, as if they were rival national giants). The Fisons' parent management really had no option but to give up this particular ghost.

Indeed, the ghost, or the spirit, of the past haunts all companies – which is another, equally strong reason for abandoning a broken base. In its heart, Fisons had stayed a fertilizer company, wedded to a market made up of farmers. It no longer has a farming stake – only £50 million of 1980 turnover in horticulture. The drug side is three times larger than that: and what was left provided a strong and large enough nucleus for Fisons to become a stock market prodigy – although in a form unrecognizable to its founders – once its management was free to manage its profitable businesses, and those alone.

The main reason for the profits lay not in any brilliance of acquisition, note, but in the successful product innovation which gave Fisons its Intal anti-asthma drug. The object of diversification is not just to give the company another line of business: but to generate the organic growth which the company requires to meet its targets and which can never be achieved from a base product that has become a base commodity. In the US, General Mills has demonstrated the right path, by investing well away from its base in flour, going for 'threshold companies', which, after the injection of money and any needed management skill by the new proprietor, have magnified exceedingly: thus thirty Red Lobster restaurants became three hundred in far faster time than if either purchaser or purchased had gone down the same route alone.

But mostly companies fall into the same context and trap as Dalgety and another flour-based firm, Spillers: the former bought the latter on the same line of reasoning that had inspired the victim's own takeovers – that the strength of the business would be increased by the very act of buying into another, unrelated, trade. The miserable experience of Spillers itself hardly endorsed the theory. Even among the sad ranks of large British companies, most of which failed to avoid actual declines in their inflation-corrected earnings per share in the decade to 1982, Spillers was a conspicuous sinner.

After deciding to escape from over-dependence on the commodities of flour and bread and compete in fast-moving consumer goods (like petfoods) against multi-national heavyweights of the Mars calibre, the Spiller management only succeeded in demonstrating year after year that it was hopelessly over-matched. It's vital to learn just where weakness in those combats proves so killing.

The Triumph of the New

The answer to this question, and the solution to the commodity threat, have been carefully documented by an expert from the A.C. Nielsen company, studying success and failure of new products introduced into the grocery trade. The failure rate is notorious – well over 90 per cent. But the majority of the rare large successes come from the largest companies: which, of course, is why they stay the largest. Part of the reason for their dominance, no doubt, is pure muscle: the financial and distributing might that gives an enormous advantage in developing and putting across something new to the consumer and the trade. But another reason is probably pure management: the giants simply take more care over their new product programmes – and, above all, they have such things.

If the Nielsen guru is correct, products that weren't around ten years ago always account for about a quarter of sales in any sector. Thus any company not developing wonders that will stay the course must eventually be shut out from more and more of its market segment. That doesn't mean developing mere line extensions or relaunches, however. These are the expedients – often very necessary – which persuade non-innovators that they are the innovative opposite.

Whether markets are fast- or slow-growing, the companies in search of higher profits and real corporate expansion are going to carry on competing, fighting the packaged goods fight with all their might. At the end of the day, global market shares may be little changed by all the moiling and toiling: though the incomes of advertising agencies, media, marketing men *et al* will be merrily inflated along the way. However, it would be a mistake to suppose that brilliant marketing and advertising alone will win the day. The race will go to the manufacturer who can produce the genuine blockbuster innovation.

Yet, to take the grocery trade again, in the 1980s innovations have been even sparser on the ground, or the shelf, than usual – witness the magazine *Supermarketing*'s 1980 list of top new products. In the main, the goodies named were by no stretch of the imagination more than stretches of the product line. Many of them must have cheerfully cannibalized sales from the main product lines from whose womb they sprang – a constant danger that, in overcrowded markets like these, will beset many coming efforts to steal a competitive march. Indeed, the prospect yawns ahead of generation after generation of

37

imitative 'me-too' and 'me-me-too-too' products.

The yawn will no doubt be shared by the consumer. The signs are that the housewife in the supermarket is getting more selective, more bored with sameness, in which she is no different from any other consumer in any other emporium. 'Me-too' is a sure way of guaranteeing that products will turn into commodities. 'Me-different' is the only hope for any company which wishes to win markets worth the victory. The future rests firmly and fully, not only on efficiently exploiting the old (if it is viable), but on genuine triumphs with the genuinely new.

5: The Challenge to Prestige

One company's innovation is another firm's poison – even a long-time market leader can be killed off by a technology which is a new and, by definition, unexpected threat. The exploitation of xerography by a firm (Haloid, later Xerox) outside the traditional copying industry sounded the death knell to the giants of duplicating. They have taken, true, a long time a–dying. But today the technological leaps are longer and faster: the death of those who are left behind may no longer be lingering. Like so many little old Swiss watchmakers, stranded hopelessly by the electronic watch, even the mighty and modern and prestigious are vulnerable.

It's difficult, of course, for one's heart to bleed for a company so massively successful for so many years as Kodak. But after absorbing the onslaught of Polaroid, and long putting off the evil day when it had to compete in instant photography itself, Kodak has been challenged from another and far more threatening Great Leap Forward in technology. In the 1980s the filmless camera, already fast cornering the movie market, will emerge in still photography, as Sony, Canon *et al* keep their promises (or threats): and what will Kodak do about that?

Kodak will not be alone in seeking the answer to one of marketing's most atrocious questions. The several high-prestige, high-quality camera firms in Japan which lack the necessary technology must be wondering how the new wonder will (or won't) affect them. The strategic choices start with the Do-Nothing Deal, otherwise known as the Ostrich Theory; or, if you shut your eyes Sony will go away; or, its Mavica camera won't work well (at the initial stage, apparently, the colour version didn't); or, people won't want to buy it. The trouble with this head–in–the–sand approach is that, while dead easy and involving no capital expenditure, it may be fatally wrong.

A more sophisticated version is to do nothing, but get some hasty research and development under way, so that, if the new competitor does take off, you can dive in quick before all the water has been drained from the pool. In Kodak's case, the problem is not that camera sales will be lost (since Kodak serves the mass market, and the Mavica will start dear), but that film sales might be threatened. When Polaroid came along it was easier for Kodak to hedge its bets, since it made the film for its new rival, until the latter unwisely pulled the plug. But if you haven't got Sony's technology in-house already, what are Kodak's hopes as it strives to catch up in so advanced a field as electronics?

A similar question hangs ominously over the opposite policy from Do-Nothing, which is to throw every available resource into beating the competitor to the punch. The chances of success are so remote that it makes more sense to follow the General Motors example, and buy rights to a new wonder (as it did with the Wankel engine) in order to protect your flanks. You then run the risk of finding out expensively and too late, as did GM, that Do-Nothing would have worked best, because the enemy did in fact disappear before your very eyes.

In other words, there is no easy solution. But there is a certainty: that no company occupying an important position in any market should neglect any challenge, trivial or tremendous, that threatens any part of its market stature. In this particular case, Kodak would certainly have been unwise to take much notice of Sony's Akio Morita when he said his system was unlikely to replace conventional photography. No doubt that's what they said about valves when the first transistor radio was launched.

One leading US manufacturer, Zenith, even for a while used its old-fashioned design as a selling point – none of this new-fangled nonsense. But new-fangledness tends not only to win: it takes the bread from the mouths of the old-fangled. Thus RCA, which dominated the vacuum tube business, missed the transistor boat and never got back on board. Kodak is trying desperately hard not to repeat an error which would be fatal in a company much less diversified than RCA. Hence the massive research effort to turn the Rochester stalwart into an electronic-based rather than a film-based company.

In other words, Kodak cannot live off its technological past if it wants to have a future – even if the future is problematical. After all, nobody was to know that instant photography would be contained by developments in conventional cameras. The battle might have gone the other way: and so might Kodak – down.

The Lessons of the Laser

Take the similar situation when the laser audio disc was unveiled, again by Sony, this time with Philips. Would or wouldn't the disc do to the conventional long-playing record what the latter had done to the 78? The arrival of the laser disc raises some fascinating management questions. Launching a new technology can carry serious marketing risks. If the revolutionary innovation gets out of hand, it can, like any successful revolution, destroy the established order for keeps – though, for sure, there were adding machine and slide rule manufacturers who didn't see the first, large, expensive electronic calculators as any threat at all.

What if the laser disc did make the long-playing disc as redundant as the piles of 78s now littering so many attics? Would they be joined by mouldering turntables, ranging from the Linn Sondek (£402, without pick-up arm at that) to the down-market machines of Sony and Philips themselves? If these stirring events came to pass, what would be the impact on record companies other than Philips, or on turntable, arm and cartridge makers outside the big names backing the compact disc system? And would laser discs bring the relentless advance of the cassette to a grinding halt?

For a technological challenge to subvert a market, there must be a real advantage, in price or in use, over the existing product. While the discs are almost as compact as cassettes, they lack the disadvantages of hiss, fragile tapes and unreliable reproduction. On the other hand (which is characteristic of new technologies in their first manifestation) the discs (like the players in relation to those for LPs) started out very expensive compared to cassettes.

The latter's cheapness, of course, is what damaged record sales so severely – down by 30 per cent since 1975 – as do-it-yourself pirates pinched music off the air or other people's discs. To that extent, laser discs offered the record industry a golden hope of winning back the lost customers. But wait: any bonanza of that kind depends not only on a vast increase in the library of compact discs available, but also on contradicting the basic marketing strategy by which innovators try to restrict the damage done by the new technology.

That strategy is to price the miracle product at the very top of the market, and then to bring the price down gradually over time as the market widens. So long as costs (thanks to the combined wonders of the learning curve and economies of scale) fall faster than prices, everything in the garden is lovely. Thus the Philips players weighed in initially at Linn Sondek levels of £499; the more sophisticated Sony cost a cool £549; while buying all the 5-inch discs (£8 to £10 for an hour of playing) then available would have cost £1,600 to £2,000.

In the past this strategy has worked well, in celebrated examples from nylon stockings to Polaroid cameras. But the pace of technological life has been hotting up – witness the frenetic multiplication and price falls in microelectronics, both components and computers alike. Assuming that the laser disc really is the great advance claimed in quality, durability, and desirability – a steel–radial tyre (which stole the market) rather than a Corfam synthetic leather (which flopped) – it's hard to see its exclusivity lasting much longer than that of the first expensive quartz watches. In which case, somebody, somewhere, is going to share the sad fate of those little old Swiss watchmakers already mentioned.

No Prestige Without Profits

There is a defence to which companies under attack often turn: like Zenith (or big old Swiss watchmakers such as Omega, Rolex and Patek Philippe) they can cling to the liferaft of high quality and high prestige. It can be a bumpy ride. In 1982 Zenith made a $22 million loss, having rewarded its shareholders with a 4 per cent annual decline in the investment since 1972. The truth is that technological superiority and superior prestige cannot be divorced for more than a moment; nor prestige from prestigious management.

To put it another way, if higher prestige doesn't pay off in higher profits, it isn't worth much. The essence of the situation was exemplified when Lord Forte's effort to capture Savoy Hotels was at its most intense. The directors of the latter may have known more than Forte about running de luxe hotels (though you shouldn't bet on it): but when it came to managing a business, the record spoke (or rather whimpered) for itself. In 1970, when turnover was two–thirds lower, the Savoy group made twice as much profit as it did nine years later. If Forte's Waldorf, just across the Strand, had performed so feebly, either the hotel or its managers would have been put out to grass long before.

To the then chairman Sir Hugh Wontner, for whom the Savoy was 'an historic part of London that it is my duty to preserve', that may have been beside the point. Prestige, however, isn't its own reward; even though the managers of prestige products do commonly behave as though high prestige necessarily equates with low profits – if any. No doubt that thought consoled the managers of the Rolls-Royce car division, during the dozen years of losses before their large and mounting profits, as an independent company, exposed the unflattering truth of the previous incompetence.

Of course, prestige is in itself a mighty marketing asset. The money-losing Rolls-Royce still commanded the reputation of making 'the best car in the world': even after auto *aficionados* had long ceased to think it anything of the sort. But if management itself still believes in the former glories, great danger threatens.

Indeed, Rolls-Royce sales did drop alarmingly, especially in the key US market, when the buyers who made that market decided that the machine was too little car for the money being asked, thus forcing the company into the unprecedented step of slashing its prices to salvage its sales. Prestige, like advertising, is ultimately only as good as the product. More: like any other factor in management, prestige is not priceless. It has a cost, and that cost must be abundantly covered by the returns. Otherwise you stumble into the Savoy Syndrome: with losses in four of the ten years 1973–82, and post-tax returns on capital never out of single figures – usually low ones.

The larger the loveliness of the product (or themselves) looms in the managerial minds, the greater the chance that non-prestigious, mundane matters will be ignored – like the management, control and marketing systems in which Forte is expert. Those proficient systems partly explain why Sir Charles, who was once 'practically nothing', just as Wontner said, came to control a group with, in 1979, some 27 times the sales and 133 times the profits of the Savoy Group: that's really something.

Prestige implies premium quality and premium prices – and from the latter, the well-managed company should derive a premium profit. That trick in turn demands, in some respects, even tighter,

43

tougher management than does serving the mass market: because the prestige business is vulnerable not only to lower-priced or more efficient competition (witness the Japanese camera firms which undercut and overtook the lordly Leica), but to management's own potentially poor sense of priorities. Often, prestige goeth before a fall. The true prestige lies in truly being Number One: and that demands primacy in all respects. In that position, a company has options. Once you lose primacy, in technology or anything else, the options rapidly begin to disappear.

6: Where Biggest Is Best

Genuine top quality which generates genuine top prestige reinforces its owner by creating something else: top branding. The car industry provides classic proofs, both negative and positive, of the role of the brand in markets. Long-running failures (although by definition they don't run for ever) have failed brand policies. But no long-running market success demonstrates more convincingly the vital relationship between product, image, label, and marketing performance than the might of Mercedes-Benz. In the post-1973 decade, even in a West Germany whose manufacturers were mostly sunk in shocked gloom, which recession usually produces in their unaccustomed minds, Mercedes drove further ahead. Its continuing rise in sales and production for the awful car year of 1982 was the stuff of which most other car groups' dreams were made: for the next year, the company grew still further, proving again the power of a formula strong in its very simplicity.

Once it had re-established its technical reputation post-war with a famous string of racing triumphs, Mercedes consolidated its position at the top of the market. It has concentrated on making up-market machines that are consistent in performance and image: solid, reliable, fast, comfortable, and unmistakably Mercedes in style down to the last knob. Subordinate branding of individual models has been minimal. For example, while a recent new range incorporated enough engineering improvements to enthuse the experts and had also been given (by restrained Mercedes standards) a significant face-lift as well, it wasn't granted a series letter to itself – it was the *new* S series.

The company's totally novel introductions come at rare, long intervals, which helps again to confirm the image of stability and consistency. Coupled with methodical and highly effective build-up of distribution, the steadiness has brought Mercedes unexampled volume for a luxury producer. Its 1982 and 1983 worldwide sales were over two-thirds those of all British-made cars on the UK market in the same two years – the German firm turned out more than 450,000 motors in the two years combined. As an article in *Management Today* pointed out, British firms in many industries have shunned volume business to go after up-market segments with higher added value and higher quality – but they may have barked up the wrong tree: the great Japanese success stories (just like Mercedes) achieve those triumphs by *combining* quality and volume.

Another lesson is that building on an established segment (like luxury executive transport) is as important as finding it in the first place. Mercedes had its strokes of good fortune here – such as being the leading maker of diesel cars when the oil crisis struck. But it also masterfully surmounted its apparent vulnerability, as a company making only gas-guzzlers in a fuel economy era – and that was before the appearance of the down-sized range that was its main innovation of the early 1980s and the latest, most severe challenge to its marketing skills.

But what are those skills? They don't lie in the aggressive promotion and clever identification of 'niches' that have made BMW another fine example of German marketing power in the same industry. The Mercedes skill rests on the persistent projection and reinforcement of a high-quality, one-brand product: and nothing in marketing works better. The brand is the brilliance, and the brilliance is the brand.

The Product Death-Cycle

Neglect the brand, and you neglect the product – and neglect has been the largest single cause of brand and product death. Modern marketing has discovered that, by and large, products don't die: they are killed, the victims of managers who have either fallen for discredited concepts, like the inevitability of the product life-cycle (the death-cycle is a better phrase), or who have just fallen asleep. There are exceptions, true, one of them mentioned in Chapter 1. If you're marketing a drug like Opren, which might be killing patients, you have no option but to kill the drug – which gives another twist to that phrase 'death-cycle'. But in the majority of cases, product death is involuntary euthanasia.

The car industry offers no starker constrast to Mercedes-Benz than Standard-Triumph. Once a company with a respectable share of the British market, it launched a whole series of perfectly sound cars (the Vanguard, the Herald, the 2000, the Dolomite, the Spitfire, the TR sports series, etc). With the exception of the TRs, not one of these offerings received the progressive, planned development that Ford automatically and so successfully gave to its Cortinas, Escorts, and so on. For lack of this brand nourishment, Triumph's tale proceeded inexorably to a sad finish – the brand or badge was adorning only one product from BL's factories, a borrowed Japanese design, when its doom was pronounced in February 1984.

This rake's progress had no rational explanation. The logic behind Ford's model programme (new body every four years, new engine every seven) was as obvious as the marketing muscle put behind both the corporate brand (Ford) and the model brand (Cortina, Escort, Capri, etc.). The apparent total absence of thought at Triumph has only one, very poor, excuse – its procedure was the norm among British car manufacturers.

The brand development problem bedevilled BL as a whole in all its corporate forms (British Motor Corporation, British Leyland, BL). Originally, the idea was to develop the company as a mini-General Motors, or at least a Mercedes-Benz, strong in both commercial vehicles and cars, with a distinctive stance in the marketplace. The object was to establish a credible and enduring world presence. Britain alone was obviously insufficient, especially given the strong domestic competition from the major forces of GM and Ford, both desperate for non-US sales, adding to the competitive weight deployed in the UK market from Japan and Europe. To succeed, BL needed not only the models of which it was crucially short for years, but also the clear brand identities which past mis-marketing (as at Triumph) had wantonly destroyed.

In volume cars, the old generic brands ran out of life: until Austin and Morris, once huge pullers, hardly sang in the mind. BL was thus forced back on straight model branding: Mini, Metro (or was it Mini-Metro? The confusion persisted), Ital, Princess, with Bounty and others ahead. The same fate befell Vauxhall before its dramatic turnaround in the early 1980s: Viva, Victor, Chevette, Royale, etc. –

47

all came and sometimes went, without leaving any lasting family brand strength on which GM's hard-pressed British operation could rely. In the UK crumbling of Chrysler, under British, American, and French management in turn, exactly the same phenomenon occurred.

No doubt the weak branding reflected ill-considered marketing strategy, for Britain's volume car marketers have mostly been uncertain of their positioning – although the logic for BL has always been that, with small volumes in a mass market, the supplier must go for high prices. The latter, though, are impossible to command without building a high reputation for engineering excellence, quality, and style into a strongly supported brand image. The Metro, Maestro and Montego have to establish their branded merits, by systematic, organized, planned, and methodical reinforcement, refreshment and repair: that way the product can live, not for ever, but for a long and lucrative life.

The Business of the Brand

These essentials of a product/brand policy are probably easier to apply if product, brand, and company are one and the same. In that respect, an IBM has the edge over a GM. It's far harder to maintain corporate branding over a widely diverse product range, or one in which (as with GM) the company is competing with itself. In that case, the brand becomes in effect a separate firm: which may have unfortunate results.

That kind of misfortune explains why GM started totally reshaping itself, in its most radical revision since the pre-war, founding days of Alfred P. Sloan. Its existing brand pattern simply didn't fit the evolution of its markets. For the last phrase, read 'the rise of the Japanese'. Without the challenge from the East, the GM organization might well have lasted to the end of the century. But even with stiff quota restrictions, the Japanese share of the US market had risen to about 21 per cent. While GM dominated sales of US-made cars almost as never before (with around three-fifths), not only was it unable to roll back the Eastern tide of small cars by straight competition: it couldn't even come near the costs in Toyota City.

In 1983 both Toyota and Nissan had US sales comfortably over the half a million mark where VW peaked; the Germans were selling only a third of these Japanese figures, having staged one of the more sensational sales collapses in car history. GM hadn't done likewise: but its small cars had limped in the Japanese wake partly because all five famous brand divisions (Chevrolet, Buick, Pontiac, Oldsmobile, and even Cadillac) had covered the waterfront, from full-sized to down-sized. In the process, GM moved nearer and nearer to what the British deprecate as 'badge engineering', with different names on more or less identical cars.

GM's real engineering was all done centrally, anyway: until previous reforms, under the long-running GM rethink and fight-back, the divisional marketers had no real responsibility for the models they had to sell. That, of course, is marketing nonsense literally of the first order. The further stage of GM's revolution meant bifurcating the colossus: with Chevrolet and Pontiac forming a sub-company (still of gigantic size) to look after smaller cars from conception to consummation, and leaving the larger models to the other brands.

GM's marketing managements face a fascinating task in preserving their branding (and dealer networks) while reshuffling the products which the latter support. But it's hard to see that GM had any option: even if your resources are gigantic, these days they have to be concentrated to guarantee, not success, but the possibility of success in an environment where branding weakness of any kind may be fatal.

More successful multi-brand strategies than GM's abound in fast-moving consumer goods, in fact. Thus, Beecham's corporate name is carried only by a single product line among many. But Macleans, a major toothpaste for decades, was one of the original constituents in the Beecham's merger: and the marketing management has missed very few tricks in up-dating the brand to match the twists and turns of the market, even while (with Aquafresh) attacking brilliantly with an entirely new brand both in Britain and the US. Innovating assaults like Aquafresh capture the imagination as they make their initial penetration: but launch is only a start. The race is won not by speed of the mark, but by staying power.

That is one reason why the companies with most established market leaders are also those which win the prizes for new product development – companies like Lever Brothers, Pedigree Petfood, Kellogg and P & G. These champions adhere to what the great management prophet, Lyndall F. Urwick, set out as a marketing catechism in 1933: paying successful attention to things like 'constant and systematic study of the products and methods of competitors',

49

'the development of new avenues and methods of distribution', 'the supply of new products . . . to secure the established market and the winning of new markets'.

Of course, life isn't always like that. Success as well as failure can sometimes drop from the skies. For example, the smash hit of Stowells' Wine Box sprang from somebody's visit to Australia, where this minor marvel of modern technology was developed. The story goes that success caught everybody unawares. Having bought the necessary machinery, etc., the Stowells men presented a small ad agency, which then had the account, with a blank white box and nothing else. If a marketing budget or any idea of the market potential existed, they were not communicated to the creative people at the agency. Their clever design, however, treated the Box as a poster, which is how it worked when gracing the off-licences.

Initially, that's all the Box did grace – there was no promotion expenditure. Only as the Box took off into the marketing blue (thus proving, incidentally, the great and sadly under-rated power of packaging) was the marketing budget lifted with it. Any honest marketing manager can produce such examples of triumphs (rather than Triumphs) which in hindsight look like marvels of mental might and rational decisions, but which actually swooped up on him unawares.

But unawares may be unaware. Stowells itself didn't capture the public imagination: that was done by the product concept, Wine-in-a-Box, promptly copied with the speed of light by all competitors with the necessary wit and resources. The innovator had missed the chance of killing two, if not three, birds with one stone: winning both market leadership for its boxed wines and a huge leap in recognition of Stowells as both a brand and a retail chain. Probably few customers know that it is the wine and spirits outlet of Whitbread's, which (in common with all the major brewers) has used a wine name as far removed from beer and pubs as possible.

Whether that's right is doubtful – but it's beyond doubt that the brewers have put far more effort behind their beer branding than behind their wine and spirits business. That in turn, no doubt, reflects internal orientations more than any considered assessment of the market. In much the same way, internal orientation explains why Distillers (DCL), the Scotch king, has lost momentum in world markets over not just a few years, but over the decades since pioneers like the afore-mentioned Lyn Urwick told managers how to market.

To take the last ten years alone, in 1974 a small company called Arthur Bell and Sons turned over £60 million, a mere ninth of the mammoth's total. In 1982–3, after multiplying fourfold, Bell's had reached a fifth of DCL's sales. As for profits, the one-time tiny tot had increased its net earnings 832 per cent over a period in which DCL's trebled. Yet despite the erosion of its share in key markets by essentially one-product companies like Bell's, the giant had a formidable portfolio of brands which, given aggressive and ambitious modern marketing, could surely wreak on its smaller rivals the havoc that IBM has visited on its lesser foes.

When you think that Bell's originally launched its sensational rise on the slogans 'Afore ye go' and 'Have a ting-a-ling', you can see that DCL's whisky barons can't exactly have been awake at the switch. Hence the great DCL shake-up in a belated uphill struggle to drag the whisky barons out of feudal marketing and into some semblance of modern times. As noted, General Motors has set in motion the greatest reshuffle in its history to sharpen its fightback against the Japanese and to recover lost brand identity – and there are obvious analogies between Scotch and cars in this instance.

Whatever DCL's brands stood for in the past, they didn't any more. Whatever sense it once made to have separate companies marketing separate, ill-differentiated brands in all geographical markets, it didn't make sense any more. Hence the necessity for a clear split of overseas and home trade. Hence, too, the eminently sound £250 million bid for Somerset, the US distributor of Johnnie Walker. One reason for Scotch reversals in that vital American market is that the distillers didn't control their own distribution – which has become increasingly deadly in the battle of the US brands (not just in liquor, either). The past neglect of Urwick's principles by DCL over fifty years explains its brands' loss of eminence – and demonstrates that quality and prestige alone cannot support a brand. That vital task demands organization, governing will, and dominating purpose.

Heller's Golden Rules

HOW TO . . .

. . . SUSTAIN GROWTH
1: Go for market pull, not technology push
2: Remember that wonder-products always cease
3: Build products into product-portfolios

. . . INNOVATE SUCCESSFULLY
1: Match innovation with administration and production
2: Innovate on the broadest possible front
3: Never forget that production is sales is design is marketing

. . . MAKE MONEY
1: Match the marketing process to the promise
2: Get the most from the least – not from the most
3: Don't identify marketing success with public impact and awareness

. . . AVOID COMMODITIES
1: Know that commodity products are made, not born
2: Turn commodities into products by moving upwards
3: Diversify to develop organic growth
4: Innovate or die: me-different is the best hope

. . . MEET CHALLENGE
1: Don't just stand there, do something
2: Remember that technological exclusivity doesn't last
3: Equate true prestige with premium quality, prices and profits

. . . BUILD BRANDS
1: Combine quality and volume
2: Support brands by systematic organization, and planned and methodical reinforcement, refreshment and repair
3: Don't think that quality and prestige alone can defend a market

SECTION TWO
FOCUS

1: I Know What They Like

Victory in the naked market demands more organized management, and better managed organizations, than ever before. The necessity of method, however, by no means excludes the primacy of ideas – of inspirations which may well be born, not from the intellect, but from the gut. Most, if not all, supreme marketing triumphs, from Ford to Sony, have sprung from the particular, instructive, intuitive identification of a taste or interest (usually that of one person, a Henry Ford I or an Akio Morita) with those of a great, fat mass market.

Indeed, the most valuable talent in marketing, the one gift which the doting marketing parent would wish for his infant, is clearly that: an unfailing instinct for what the customers want. The licences to print money go to those who sense or guess consumer tastes before anybody else – and who know how to gratify and satisfy the same: like, in the world of the media, the late Lord Thomson (commercial TV and newspapers), or Lord Grade, formerly of ACC (which as ATV was the prime mover in British commercial TV).

The trouble with tastes, though, is not only that they change, but that the markets in which the tastes are met change as well. Once upon a time ATV and its US equivalents could concentrate on churning out their recipes in a simple mono-product format – network television. Now, in the age of the multi-media conglomerate, with the media still multiplying, nothing is that straightforward. Lord Grade at least had the vision to sense the change: hence his own conglomerate ventures into White Men's Graves like feature films. What he didn't have was one irreplaceable quality: youth.

Marketing knows precious few cases either of middle-aged (let alone aged) breakthroughs, or of maestros who, like the old man of

Spain in the limerick, can do it again and again. Rather, that's what's wrong – they do repeat and repeat the winning formulae of the past, until they arrive at the point where the recipe no longer works. If they continue to stick (literally) around, the results for their companies are generally excruciating: the longevity of the Hollywood tycoons helped to ensure that their creations, MGM, Paramount, Twentieth Century-Fox, and so on all ended up as mere divisions of somebody else's conglomerate.

Taste-making and sensing are really a young man's game. Careers which only start in middle age (as with the above-mentioned Roy Thomson's breakout into Canadian radio) are as rare as the white rhino. The predominance of relative youth makes it important to have a management structure which, at the right time, allows the young people to make the running: like the persistent Sony executive who, unable to persuade his seniors, could still get through to president Morita with the marvellous idea of the personal hi-fi.

But it's rare to find a boss of Morita's stature who will listen to and back (against opposition) the inspirations of younger people: rarer still to find an entrepreneurial tycoon, used to years of the applause of the multitude, who can bear to change his own act. The absurd incident at ACC, when an executive committee specifically excluding Lord Grade was formed, had an exact parallel in the last days of the late great electrical tycoon, Sir Jules Thorn: another case where the tycoon had outlived his touch.

The problem (as shown by the events which culminated in ACC's takeover and Grade's ousting) is to deal with the problem – before it metastases into a crisis. For the flash of the old brilliance (the Muppets, which Lew Grade brilliantly spotted and backed) you pay (heavily) with the dull thud of the new fallibility (*Raise the Titanic*). The problem thus gets resolved finally by failure – but only after enormous damage has been done to the image of the company in the marketplace. It makes a strong case for compulsory retirement at sixty-five, if not sixty. After all, at seventy-five a man is older than nearly all his market: and anybody who thinks that doesn't matter doesn't know marketing.

It isn't just a question of the much-trumpeted youth market: although fate isn't merely tempted, but positively enticed, by middle-aged executives who think they understand nymphets and moppets. The need is to be in tune with the spirit of the age and the technology

55

of the times. The tender years of people like Steven Jobs, the Apple computer founder, are no accident. Nor is it any accident that the large companies in the high-technology industries have found it very hard to retain the Jobs-like talents in their suffocating bosoms. Brilliant breakthroughs are more commonly found where the genius has personal motivation to make his idea succeed, and personal responsibility for the plan's progress from birth to realization.

Why Government Gets It Wrong

The genius can be corporate as well as individual. Witness the sharp contrast between the fate of schemes where the ideas and ambitions of companies have been subordinated to government intervention, or where the whole idea springs from the infertile mind of government. The remarkable triple tragedy of Hawker-Siddeley is an ironic example. It's not often that a stunning marketing success is a source of immediate grief for its progenitors. But the US triumph of the Hawk jet trainer, when the Pentagon placed a huge order for the aircraft, while great news for British Aerospace, was only a £300 million might-have-been for Hawker-Siddeley – it launched the plane only to see its aircraft interests nationalized (by one vote in the House of Commons).

The Hawk, the Harrier jump-jet and the British participation in the A300 Airbus are all jewels in British Aerospace's crown – and all Hawker projects. The critical point, however, is that all three were launched as private ventures, or PVs: not because Hawker was at all averse to public money, but because in all three cases the government originally didn't want to know. For instance, the whole concept of the Hawk, with the insistence that it be a tactical aircraft as well as a trainer, was the manufacturer's idea of what the customer needed, not the customer's.

Why is this particular customer nearly always wrong? The record of government-backed ventures, in aerospace or anything else, is one of failure so nearly complete as to defy the law of averages. Add to the sins of commission those of omission (like the obtuse decisions not to back the three Hawker PVs), and there is plainly a great mystery to resolve. It can't simply be because the government is offered only the duff projects that nobody else will finance – the Hawker PVs alone contradict that thesis.

Perhaps the question is better approached the other way round: why did Hawker get it right? Part of the answer is that the company's future in the aviation industry depended absolutely on correct market predictions and projections. On the customer's side, the mistakes didn't matter. Nobody's future in government would have suffered if Britain had missed the Airbus; or if the jump-jet had been permanently grounded; or if the Hawker management hadn't negotiated so tight a Harrier deal with McDonnell-Douglas, guaranteeing over a third of the work on its planes for the UK factories.

Yet the mistakes would have mattered considerably, for the nation if not for those responsible, had Hawker not proceeded privately, putting its money where its market was. The story rubs in that ancient management truth mentioned above, that you only get the best performance where those responsible for policy are also charged with its execution. No doubt, the bureaucrats who turned thumbs-down on the three PVs took some kind of view on the future markets for British aerospace products. But they weren't properly equipped to do so: and so they got it wrong.

By an irony of fate, their governmental successors got the projects anyway – lock, stock, and barrel. But that demonstrates nothing. The lasting moral of the story is that even those who form the market – and the Ministry of Defence is Britain's only domestic customer for weapons systems – may well have a worse idea of what the market needs than the man or men who must live from and off the market.

Marketing Smarts Call the Tune

That by no means justifies a jump to the conclusion that market research is futile. It is – if the researcher asks hypothetical questions, like 'Would you like such-and-such a product if it existed?' Or 'What isn't on the market that you'd like?' Iffy questions get iffy answers. Research is indispensable for testing a real, hard product concept, or for finding possibly invaluable explanations for market phenomena.

As an example, take the boom in compact 35 mm cameras, a sector previously in so sharp a decline that manufacturers had given it up for dying. Then somebody in Japan had the wit to ask why: why were sales falling? The answers (difficult loading, complex operations, the need to focus, etc.) established the idea of the auto-focus, auto-exposure, auto-loading, auto-wind camera with automatic built-in

57

flash – and, hey presto, sales started to boom by 50 per cent per annum, changing the whole shape of the market.

In other words, the manufacturers had got out of step with their market. The auto-focusing mechanism which keeps the rare genius in constant communion with his customers is not only the exception that proves no rules: in complex, segmented markets this kind of lightning is unlikely to go on striking in the same place. Continuous, organized questioning and questing are the indispensable methodology – and variants and variations are the objects of the search. The single-product, single-brand king of the market, with its dominance resting on the one dominant theme, has joined the dodo. What an old-line giant like Coca-Cola has been forced to do (proliferate brand variations and innovations to defend its lead against Pepsi) is precisely the same course enjoined on an indecently young market-leader like Apple.

The latter, as noted in Chapter 1, turned to Pepsico for a new chief executive, John Sculley, in the certain knowledge that, without a powerful injection of professional marketing management, it might well fall victim to a potentially virulent strain of the De Soto disease. For those to whom De Soto means nothing, that is precisely the point. It was one of the myriad motor companies that boomed in the industry's early days and then disappeared, by amalgamation or death, as the pressure of the heavyweights become inexorable. In Apple's case, the hard-pressing mammoth is the heaviest of them all – IBM. Even without the impact of IBM's brand power and marketing muscle, taking a third of total personal computer sales in no time at all, Apple would have been increasingly squeezed: IBM's stockwave has made the pressure trebly intense.

Its success has stimulated the second largest computer company, DEC, to intensify its cultivation of Apple's orchard, along with other technological power-houses like Hewlett-Packard, Wang, and Data-General. Throw in the fact that the Japanese are thrusting powerfully for sales, and that US rivals who grew spectacularly along with Apple (like Commodore) are still in business, and you have a marketing maelstrom. De Sotoism has set in, as smaller stars like Vector and Osborne have dimmed after only a few years of glorious life.

Apple's hopes of avoiding similarly inglorious retrenchment can no longer rest on the identification of its founding Steves, Jobs and Wozniak, with a market composed of like-minded computer buffs.

Actually, it never did. The key to Apple's triumph was the machine's adoption by managers as a business tool, a development which Jobs and his backers had the wit and wisdom to exploit at full speed ahead. The exploitation of Apple's friendly name and image was also a highly professional demonstration of the marketing skills that were truly required to turn the Jobs' genius into hard sales.

But the hard truth, even while the Apple II was still pouring off the assembly lines at one every fifteen seconds, was that a one-Apple company was no more viable than a one-Coke corporation. To maintain itself as a billion-dollar business the infant Apple (b. 1976) had to sell, not a computer, but a whole range of products, distributed and supported in the marketplace as impartially as, well, apples – or Pepsi. In today's high-competition markets, high technology is of the highest importance: but it is not the highest protection. That stems from keeping the two halves of the vital equation, the market and the man (or the management), in touch. Getting out of touch is the marketing sin that's unforgiveable at any time: difficult to cure at most times: and, if unhealed, fatal in these times, when technology may set the tempo, but it's those marketing smarts which call the tune.

2: They Know What They Like – And That's All

Once upon a time there was an American professor who believed that the manifest destiny of the world economy was to be controlled by 300 giant multi-national corporations. Now that he has been proved manifestly wrong, it's important for marketing managements to understand why – because the answer lies deeply rooted, not just in the nature of huge corporations, but in that of the fast-evolving markets of today.

Take, as a demonstration of the processes at work, the very strange case of General Motors, the world's greatest manufacturing company. You would suppose that, stuffed with management and money, GM could impose its will on any market it chose – and you would suppose wrong. In the UK, having first seen its domestic appliance business, the once market-leading Frigidaire, go down the drain, GM proceeded to record nine losses (the ninth a thumping £83.3 million) in ten years of making a comparable mess of Vauxhall.

Naturally, there are plenty of extenuating circumstances. The decade started with too small a share of Europe's most sluggish car market. Ever since the oil price crisis of 1973, too, the truck business (where Bedford used to reign supreme, but took its lumps from Ford) has travelled a bumpy road. The car side, anyway, was squeezed between the importers and Ford – and, like the latter, suffered from having its assembly operations divided in two, by government fiat, with one of the plants on Merseyside. But excuses are not explanations.

The underlying truth is that Vauxhall was never allowed by Detroit to develop its own destiny. It thus lagged fatally behind in producing its first small car: GM didn't believe in small cars. The independent design and development strength which gave Ford the first Cortina and consolidated its hold on the UK market was never really matched at Vauxhall. When the US management in Dearborn did tighten its grip on UK Ford, it was part of a bold, ultimately successful operation to create a trans-European automotive complex. GM sat on its hands across the ocean.

Then the wheel swung full cycle. GM put billions into down-sizing its cars; the design capabilities of Opel were called on to help create not just European, but world-wide answers to the Japanese challenge; the Vauxhall and Opel ranges were integrated; and the only thing wrong was that everything should have been done long before. Everybody, parent and child included, inevitably suffered from the floundering of the past.

The cost of this sad story is plain — though even the £107 million of new equity that GM had to pump into Vauxhall in a single year was a fleabite in Detroit terms. Vauxhall was too small for the Americans to manage from the US: but at GM, where everybody turns only when Father does, subsidiaries have no option but to wait their turn. What happened, when Father at long last rolled over, only demonstrated how short-sighted previous policy had been. In 1982 British industry offered few contrasts more bizarre than that between Vauxhall, with its 61 per cent rise in car output, and Ford and BL, whose production actually fell (by 10.4 per cent and 2 per cent).

The reason was not only that GM had followed its Ford leader by having a common car range sold in all the European markets and made in more than one country; nor even that it had gone a possibly decisive stage better by spreading its model ranges across the world. It was also because, descending to the local level, GM had backed the new Vauxhall models with an all-round drive to improve every aspect of performance, from labour discipline to (as noted earlier) delivering fleet cars on time. Getting your act together is not only the prerequisite of saving a sadly and long failing company — as Vauxhall was: it is, of course, the true definition of good marketing.

Marketing men notoriously brought much disillusion down on their own heads by the original emphasis, as their great day dawned, on marketing as some separate and miraculous management discipline. By the same token, many British companies, by no means only in cars, wasted their efforts (puny or not) on developing new wonders by failing to ensure that the marvels would be produced to order – or to master the little matter of not having the things fall apart in use. The point is so obvious, and so crucially important, that ignoring it is no mean achievement, of sorts.

So how and why did Vauxhall's lords ignore the imperatives of the factory floor and marketplace for so long? Again, no doubt, because even a £762 million company (1981 figures) was a drop in General Motors' $63 billion ocean. Only when setbacks in the fat and comfortable US market forced GM to see its international business as a whole did Vauxhall fall into its proper place – not as a struggling producer with an uneconomic share of a single market, but as an integral part of a broadside attack on the wide, wealthy world. The American bosses had barricaded themselves from reality with fixed ideas like 'There's no future in small cars' and 'You can't sell the same car in Britain and Germany' (let alone America). They were wrong.

The Sell-Off Phenomenon

The most conspicuously large company in the world is inevitably a conspicuous example: but conspicuous companies are the best examples of the difficulties which arise when managers try to make markets behave to suit their (the managers') convenience: when the whole point of markets is that they suit nobody's convenience, but behave as they wish. Yet even some highly sophisticated managements appear to miss the direction of markets altogether. It doesn't require punditry to prove the point: the giants prove it themselves by selling the businesses with whose markets they haven't come to terms.

One such case is the 1981 sell-off by the Dutch Philips super-mammoth of Cambridge Electronic Industries. At the time, true, it was fashionable for giants to offload bits and pieces which were either too small for their comfort or didn't fit into forward market plans. True, spun-off groups, forced to concentrate on their own markets, without Father watching over them, often show surprising speed. But CEI's twenty-odd companies weren't all that tiny; they shared £83 million of sales between them in markets which were right up Philips' main street: like electronics and electrical components, and defence and electronic systems.

Possibly, Philips never did really want these odds and sods that came in with Pye, whose previous magpie management cared not, apparently, for the economies of scale or the virtues of concentration. From that angle, the sell-off was merely the culmination of a Pye takeover which must have given the Dutch at least as much trouble as it was worth. But it seems characteristic of Philips to devote endless time and trouble to its various enterprises without in the end obtaining full pay-off from its endeavours.

Just try, for example, to think of any consumer market where Philips is the undisputed leader. No doubt there are some; in audio and video, however, Philips may or may not be 'simply years ahead' in its technology (as its UK ads claim), but the Dutch company is certainly years behind in its market impact. The Sony Walkman and the JVC video cassette recorders, to take just two examples, cleaned up while Philips plugged on determinedly into less rewarding adventures. Somehow the technical excellence doesn't seem to get translated into world-beating mass-market products.

According to one informant, the explanation is simple. Any Philips subsidiary, he says, can generate superb products for local consumption, and often conceals their development costs craftily in the accounts. If the official Philips range consisted of these black market innovations, even the Japanese might tremble. But when the ideas get back to the centre in Eindhoven, Father says no – for instance, to a marvellous portable colour TV that could have given Sony a run for its money. If this account is correct, then perhaps Eindhoven gave the wrong Philips division its freedom. Maybe all its divisions needed to be set free – not just the Cambridge ragbag.

The same sell-off phenomenon has been demonstrated by two British giants which flogged unwanted famous names in the very same week of 1983. The cases differ. GEC came by its sell-off, Morphy-Richards, via a tortuous, unplanned takeover route (the small appliance company originally belonged to EMI). Imperial Group, on the other hand, barged into the chicken business in regal, deliberate style, buying its sold company, J.B. Eastwood, et al as part of its Grand Strategy of reducing dependence on the demon tobacco. But there is a lowest common denominator. Neither great company could make the most of these assets.

That is, of course, no difficult trick if, like Imps, you pay too much for the wrong company at the wrong time – a malpractice to which tobacco barons, on both sides of the Atlantic, seem as addicted as they are to nicotine. But Imps also had huge problems in developing a management style which could generate satisfactory returns from such massive diversifications into unfamiliar pastures.

The common thread was supposed to be marketing: but the talents and techniques honed on Players No.6, say, turned out to have little direct relevance to broiler chickens and other fodder. While consumer marketers do have a common language, that lingo is general; but the management of marketing companies is inevitably highly specific – and involves far more activity, geared to the particular product and market, than sharp-end marketing alone. Above all, success demands the determination to win, the driving will that has been the missing Imps ingredient.

Nobody can even remotely accuse the Weinstock regime at GEC of lacking either an effective management style or the necessary will to win. Yet the group's vastly successful overall performance has nearly always contrasted sadly with its domestic electrical side. Right from its start, despite all its efforts, the new-look GEC, in a UK market that has provided rich diets for the Japanese and the Continentals, has never had much of a consumer feast.

The explanation may well lie in that same matter of style. The industrial and defence markets where GEC has created so much wealth do not have the vital fashion element of consumer durables; nor do new industrial products often carry the same inescapable risks as consumer innovation. Fall behind in that innovation, though, and you fail: though a widely spread giant's resources will absorb the failure easily enough. That is why the private companies to which GEC and Imps sold their unwanted offspring had a better chance of success – because they have nothing to break their concentration, and everything to lose, if break it does.

The Fix Is Father's Fault

There's another example of big company problems in the sterling efforts which Raleigh, the bicycle subsidiary inside the TI conglomerate, has made to resurrect an all-but-moribund business. In the process, it ran into attack from the Monopolies and Mergers Commission at the very nadir, when its business was in the thick of a parlous recession. The management could justifiably feel that political insult was being added to economic injury. After all, Raleigh's alleged naughtiness in refusing to supply discount houses arose from laudable attempts to preserve its faltering trade by strengthening its main retail networks. Yet there is a sense in which Raleigh's injuries are self-inflicted, and perhaps by no fault of the managers concerned: because they are stuck firmly in the bicycle shed.

In entrepreneurial marketing the manager needs to know three critical things: when to start, when to stick — and when to stop. More often than not, that's what separates the entrepreneurial sheep from the managerial goats. The entrepreneur knows, sometimes by pure instinct, when opportunity has knocked. He also knows when to stick with it during the dark hours, days, and years when labour is rewarded with nothing but losses. Finally, though, he knows when to abandon a permanently losing cause. Such decisions usually come more easily to the entrepreneurial soul than to the manager — who, in any event, seldom has the freedom to take the entrepreneurial decision. In the Raleigh case, the entrepreneur might well have concluded that, despite the ecological and exercise boom, the bike business would never see glad confident morning again. He might have preferred to get out altogether.

But Raleigh's business still looks too big and too long-term to abandon; so the entrepreneur might well have kept the bikes, geared down to the scale of his markets, and probably pushed up those markets, as far away from the low-priced Far Eastern competition as possible. Then he would have bought or built round this base other businesses in which the competitive pressures were lighter and the growth prospects longer — with the sky the only limit on his horizons. But managers buried inside conglomerates, such as Raleigh's TI parent, seldom, if ever, get that freedom. They can't form the ultimate, optimum strategy, they can only implement tactics — and hope that these will bring them through into the bright sunlight beyond.

If so, their success is a triumph of man over machine — over the corporate engineering which tries, because it must, to make all the parts mesh into the whole. If the cogs and wheels are themselves well engineered, well managed and financially well nourished in strong markets, the policy naturally works like a charm. The test comes, like all management tests, in adversity. And it is the business under pressure which, above all, can't afford to turn when Father turns: especially if it's Father's fault initially that the child got into its fix.

3: The Scads of Scad

How has Japan, the most hierarchical industrial society in the world, managed to escape the dead hierarchical hand? How have its equivalents of Morphy-Richards and Raleigh thrived where Westerners have wallowed? The answer is competition – of which the Western world does not have nearly enough. That was true even during the great oil price recession, when prices and profits came under severe pressure as the surviving manufacturers struggled to stay in the game. For price competition isn't the only element in competitiveness – not by any means. And the extent to which Western business is uncompetitive (or rather non-competitive) can be seen in seemingly minor events, like, say, Canon's launch of two highly automatic low-priced 35 mm Snappy cameras in 1982.

The significance doesn't lie only in the direct onslaught on a snapshot market which Kodak was trying to tie up still tighter with its new disc system. The real lesson resided in the fact that this top-quality Japanese producer had extended its range downwards, with innovative mass-market products, in the teeth of fierce, crowded competition at home. To test this truth, try counting the number of famous Japanese camera firms – you will need both hands and all digits.

In the durable industries of Britain, or the US, or Europe, two or three fingers are usually all you require. This difference is so striking in the markets where Japan has made its deepest inroads (think only of cars and hi-fi) as to question the whole galloping Western trend towards monopoly and oligopoly. McKinsey consultant Kenichi Ohmae is plainly right to attribute the competitive power of the Japanese outside Japan to this intense competitiveness inside.

The hustling and bustling seen in Japan are characteristic of all growth industries in their dynamic phase: the great car names that have long been amalgamated in the West were born in an atmosphere of just such cut and thrust. Today's amazing data processing market exhibits just the same effort and proliferation. True, many cooks can all keep alive and well more easily in kitchens that are busy and booming. But it's also true that the strenuous competitive endeavours themselves stimulate demand.

By the same token, the shrinkage of competitors and of competitive ranges in Western industry, and the concentration and reduction of innovative investment that have followed, must have contributed powerfully (or rather feebly) to the prevailing sluggishness. Paradoxically, the anti-trust laws which have played a part in keeping Japanese firms at each other's throats, instead of in each other's beds, were wished on the occupied nation by the post-war American military government. As with the single-industry union structure which the British similarly gave the West Germans, the occupiers wrought more wisely than they knew – and far more wisely than they have practised themselves.

The law, however, is not the only reason why the Japanese invaders outnumber the Western defenders in so spectacular a fashion. Where British, American, German, and French industry has tended to amalgamate and concentrate, the Japanese have been fruitful and multiplied in ways that their cultural norms encourage, but which those of the West hardly allow. Thus, even hi-fi *aficionados* can be forgiven for thinking that Aurex is a Toshiba brand name. Actually, Aurex is a separate part of the Toshiba empire, with a jealously guarded independence. In the same market, Aiwa is half-owned by Sony, but equally jealous and independent: while JVC, the VCR leader, is a 50 per cent interest of the giant Matsushita – but, again, autonomous and fierce about it. Other such cross-relationships abound in Japan. Where Western companies like to crush their domestic competition, the Japanese embrace it.

The result, for the investing company, is to foster a second source of technological and marketing ideas, while sharing, as an investor, in its success. The half-child gets the financial backing it requires to develop those technical ideas and to spread them across world markets. The consumer gets a greater variety of choice. And the Japanese economy gets some protection against the emergence of the bloated, over-centralized, slow-moving giants which have held back progress so visibly in many Western industries. The typical UK or US big (or even middling) company board demands 100 per cent even of almost nothing. Far, far better, surely, to have only half of something truly great.

Whether or not the Japanese businessman thinks consciously that way, the subconscious forces run powerfully against true takeovers of any kind. That would mean subjecting the 'spirits' of one company to another – something which is as unpleasing to the subjugator as to his victim. The corporate spirits, however, have no objection to beating the hell out of another company if the opportunity arises, which explains the courage and craft that Japanese companies bring to attacking any market that seems attractive – even if it is occupied by so powerful a company as Xerox in copiers or Toyota in cars.

But when a Ricoh or a Canon takes deadly aim at Xerox, or a Honda (against the wish of the government agency MITI) decides to break into the car market, the managements are not so foolish as to attack across the board. Typically, they search for the mighty opposition's weak point: the neglected sector where it is vulnerable. To put the process more positively, the company looks for a niche, a segment, which it can profitably exploit.

Time and again, the Japanese have found this segment beneath the colossus (giving an extra dimension of meaning to the phrase 'the soft under-belly of the giant'): cheaper and smaller copiers; cheaper and smaller cars; cheaper and smaller TVs. But whatever the actual products, the Japanese have nearly always followed the strategy contained in a marvellous market acroynym: Scad.

Segment, Concentrate and Develop

It stands for Segment, Concentrate and Develop. In markets which have themselves become far more segmented, what was always a sensible policy has become downright mandatory. What Apple exploited so brilliantly, for example, was a mere segment of the data processing market – the small business computer – which IBM had chosen (or maybe not even chosen) to ignore. By the same token, once Apple's bite into the overall computer market had become too big even for IBM's comfort, the giant wisely set up a segmented, concentrated group to develop its phenomenally successful counter-offensive.

At the opposite, regressive end of corporate life – the unwanted business – the lesson of the 'leveraged buy-out' is much the same. The bought-out business, which floundered so miserably inside its parent that the latter wished to be shot of the misery, time and again flourishes when set free: in almost all cases in a segmented market on which its management can concentrate in the sure knowledge that it's a case of develop or die.

The financial *legerdemain* of the buy-out formula is, of course, another powerful motivational factor. For instance, the ancient Royal Stafford pottery came into the hands of three managers who put up £40,000 between them for the equity, while the investor who took the rest also supplied £180,000 in loan capital (which provided the leverage). All they needed to do was continue as they had begun (moving from the hands of the receiver to sales of £1–1.5 million and profits of £50,000 in the first year), and the equity-owning managers would be certain to clean up a packet.

The help, however, rested firmly on Scad, which was forcefully applied from the start. One of the new management's first acts was to cut the range of patterns from forty to only four. Business history records very few cases where careful, rational scrutiny of a product range fails to come up with similar findings: that the company is making and marketing too many products or variations, most of which make either no contribution or an actual loss.

History also records very few cases where the management of the company (or some of its senior members) don't fight almost to the death for the right to go on losing money on the unnecessary offerings – or activities. Shining examples include the small, expensive shops which large, non-retailing companies maintain in smart locations like Bond Street or Fifth Avenue. Proposals to remove these excrescences from the balance sheet are invariably resisted by managers who are unable to offer any evidence that the shop makes any contribution to the company's image or sales that is at all commensurate with the cost.

The point, of course, is that retailing is for retailers. Two separate, though apparently contradictory, theories emphasize why this should be so. Theory One lays down that corporate cobblers should find a last and stick to it, and that businesses, even profitable ones, which don't fit the chosen pattern should cease forthwith to clutter up the company's single-minded marketing and management drive. Croda's Sir Freddie Wood expressed this fashionable theory perfectly when arguing that his chemicals group must concentrate on low-volume, high-profit specialities: since one of Croda's products, paracresol, didn't fit that definition, out it went.

Cognoscenti will recognize this approach as a toughened-up version of Ted Levitt's famous question, 'What business are you in?' It's now 'What business *don't* you want to be in?' The right-minded management approaches its range of businesses as a smart retailer looks at his range of merchandise; for instance, W.H. Smith has narrowed down to its core of books, stationery, records, newspapers and magazines, so as to achieve greater clarity of corporate image and the most profitable use of expensive shelf space.

In Smith's case, analysis and experience demonstrated the benefits of reversing the previous trend towards a wider and wider spread. It's much less easy to prove the point with a portfolio of businesses – unless, like the Coca-Cola wine operation, which was sold for what it cost ($210 million), the dropped darling was simply not earning its keep. In that event, of course, the purchaser must prove something, too: that he can turn this sow's ear into a silk purse.

Enter Theory Two. It holds that strategic acquisitions, by strengthening a company's overall market position, will raise profitability above and beyond whatever wonders are achieved with the new purchase itself. The in-phrase here is 'critical mass': thus the buyer of Coke Au Vin (the Canadian-owned giant, Seagram) immediately soared four places in the US wine league to second spot, with 11 per cent of the market. In other words, Theory Two doesn't really contradict Theory One, but reinforces it: the buyer *increases* his concentration and his profits, just as W.H. Smith, by at last adding heavily to its book space, is raising its turnover and profits.

Joining the Japanese

In retailing in general the old tendency was towards proliferation (of which variety chains and department stores were supreme examples), while the present trend is for just the kind of concentration mentioned. How else can a company hope to cope with rapidly changing consumer tastes? With increasingly heavy competition coming from new directions? With a bewildering multiplicity of strategic choices? And all against a background of profound demographic changes and slow growth.

Take just one market, toys, where the customers (kids) have been diverted from traditional outlets (toy shops) to multiples, other specialists (computer shops), etc. Children's leisure pursuits (like everybody else's) have greatly widened in range, and so have leisure products. For all that, the market is huge, with disposable income (of children) running in excess of £1.8 billion a year; tempting enough, surely – but only for those who can keep up with the times.

The fascinating point is not so much the specific factors affecting the toy trade, but the kaleidoscopic shake-up of the market; because the shake-up is being repeated in almost every marketplace in the land – if not the world. The consequences are obvious. Traditional ways of marketing have to change because markets are changing so traumatically, not only in the ways just mentioned but also in methods of distribution.

The good old distributive combination of manufacturer and retailer, with or without wholesale intervention, is still enormously powerful. It has shown a longer shelf life than most competitors, among whom traditional mail order has long been struggling, because the shop reinforces the product and its advertising, while the act of physical distribution offers rich economies of scale (missed by nearly everybody, according to the pundits, but never mind). To beat the High Street champs, contenders offering other routes must either sell more cheaply or more seductively.

That hasn't been easy: which is why conventional retailing and its discount store variants have by and large preserved their hold. The worrying question now – worrying for the dominant retailers, that is – is whether electronic shopping will pull the rug from under their feet. In theory, the electronic shopper will plug right in to his friendly shop, and the goods will be ordered and paid for in one fell swoop. But they can't be delivered electronically (not until *Star Trek* fiction becomes fact), and more manufacturers are bound to sense that, if a High Street supplier can deliver direct to the TV customer, so can they.

The mail order catalogue, too, seems sure to go electronic, which might well give this whole sector the kiss of renewed life. But whatever happens, the big winners are likely to be the big concentrators – the groups like Toys 'R' Us, Computerland, MFI, and Dixons: those who Segment, Concentrate and Develop in a way which isn't only worthy of the Japanese, but is the only way to join and beat them.

4: Why Quality Isn't Enough

Publishers are particularly prone to the notion that better quality, in and of itself, will generate commercial success. Leave aside the fact that quality in a magazine or newspaper is subjective, an unmeasurable effect in the eye of the beholder, and you're still left with a major misapprehension about markets. Producing a better *Vogue* might not be impossible: but the time and cost that would be involved in overtaking *Vogue*'s sale and attracting its advertisers, while simultaneously financing that superior quality – those are the real obstacles.

Even if *Vogue* obligingly did nothing to improve its own quality, the cost of competition would almost certainly be far too high to justify the venture financially. In other words, higher quality is the *sine qua non* of competition in this context: but it's not the factor which actually determines success. This truth emerged starkly from the dismal story of *Now!* magazine. Its proprietor, Sir James Goldsmith, remarked rightly over the corpse that consumer products often do fail, but he omitted to add that these failures mostly follow from incorrect assessments of the market.

In the case of *Now!*, the crucial point was whether such a magazine could attract enough high-class AB readers to justify the purchase of advertising space at what were high rates, judged by those charged for the colour supplements of the quality Sunday newspapers. In their ideas of what kind of circulation would achieve the desired result, the *Now!* promoters were misled by the seeming modesty of a target like a quarter of a million copies: peanuts by the standard of, well, the *Standard* evening newspaper. They overlooked the crucial question that faces any marketer: how to reach the magic numbers.

The only sure way available was TV advertising. For Goldsmith's purposes, though, TV had the well-known defect that it delivers far too diluted an audience (all TV, not just the commercial variety, has a low AB profile) at far too great a cost. *Now!* could indeed have been established by sustained exposure on ITV: but the expense would have made the £12 million which Goldsmith actually did lose pre-tax (on turnover that may not have exceeded £10 million) look like starters.

A Press campaign could have been more precisely targeted, but would have been most unlikely to deliver the required total response: a point that applies very strongly to the third possible course, direct mail. Even with a 2 per cent response rate, the mailing operation required to obtain 100,000 subscribers would be of overwhelmingly daunting proportions – and apparently it was the failure of the final direct mail foray (launched on the strength of a 1.6 per cent test response) that hammered the final nail into the *Now!* coffin. The so-called 'roll-out' as the rest of the mailing followed is said to have produced only half the test result.

All this elementary analysis could, of course, have been carried out before the baby was conceived. But no doubt its progenitors fell back on that age-old hope that the shining virtues of the product itself would suck in the demand required. That hope is the marketing equivalent of the morbid letters RIP.

Sometimes, but rarely, a product truly does astound even its producers by the size of demand which it generates: by definition, however, that will only happen when (as with the first breakthrough of the Apple II computer) the product taps a market that nobody suspected of existing – in this instance, the personal business computer; or when a well-conceived marketing plan suddenly achieves a grand slam (as with the IBM Personal Computer in overtaking the aforesaid Apple).

Even here, there is no reinforcement for the idea that the product will create its own market – not in a competitive situation. True, some products, like the Hasselblad camera, can survive for decades on limited sales at high prices earned by high quality. But in most cases (the Hasselblad certainly being one), close inspection will reveal a highly intelligent and artfully executed marketing policy. In any event, what works for Hasselblads won't work in the mass markets where most producers, by definition, must earn their keep. What calls the tune in mass markets is economics: perceived value, translated into price and related to volumes and hence to costs.

The Model Is the Message

This can be seen emphatically in the story of two down–and–out car companies – BL and Chrysler. The resurrection of the Chrysler Corporation in particular seems to prove that crippled giants can take up their beds and walk. In 1983 Chrysler actually made a profit, repaid a mountain of debt famously early, and again became a serious contender in US markets, with a range of models built cleverly enough round the basic 'K' car to compete effectively with Ford and GM.

In Chrysler's case, of course, a reluctant Washington guaranteed loans without which the company, down to its very last million on one horrendous day, would have failed. But from then on Chrysler was largely on its own. Its boss, Lee Iacocca, didn't have to bargain with politicians for further blood transfusions or worry about the political repercussions of some horribly drastic action – workforce halved; pay bill cut by $1.3 billion; sixteen plants closed (not to mention the execution of horrible foreign investments, like those in Britain).

The combined effect of this ruthless operation was an amazing drop in the break–even point, down by about half to 1.2 million cars a year. But a lower break–even is little use unless you get past it: and the key to Chrysler was that verdict of the market. Had US car buyers turned thumbs down on its price, performance, and perception package, the emperor in the White House would doubtless have done likewise. Troubled companies, great or small, can come back; but only if the customer says so.

It must be added that Chrysler was greatly helped in its comeback by the fact that Japanese competitors were fighting with one arm tied behind their backs by not very voluntary quotas. The same factor has undoubtedly been a help in BL's drive back to break–even and beyond in Britain. But even more important was a profound marketing change. Up to the appearance of its Metro, BL too often seemed to believe that the motor was the message: that people should buy its cars because they were jolly good – and British at that.

Indeed, there was and is a national fascination with the affairs of BL which seems to have waxed as the company's stature in the world car market has waned. Its marketers could always count on an orgy of coverage for any new model – each one of which has been promptly hailed as the make-or-break project for Britain's favourite car firm. With the Maestro, even the Bishop of Birmingham entered the act: although the connection between buying British ('a matter of conscience', according to the good bishop) and the Church of England seems slightly remote.

That, however, illustrates the obsession: BL went on stirring a patriotic *frisson* even among those who didn't buy its cars. Ford and Vauxhall simply don't elicit the same response (still less Talbot), and that's not because so many of their UK sales (to the British government's indignation) have been of cars manufactured on the Continent. In some subliminal way, the public senses that BL has a peculiarly central role in the fate of the British economy. What's been bad for BL truly has been bad for Britain – the halving of UK vehicle production (and exports) in the past dozen years has been the nation's most serious economic disaster.

But this dreadful setback, to which BL's production and marketing vicissitudes have contributed most, itself suggests that the patriotic motive doesn't translate easily into buying decisions. People may have a more intense emotional attitude towards one supplier than another, but they purchase for a variety of reasons, of which that emotion is only one: quality being another, which BL couldn't deploy because of inefficient production. But basically the message of the BL marketers wasn't heard because the company lacked an integrated, clearly branded line of vehicles, produced in sufficient volume to set against a Ford line-up which has applied the necessary basic principles for two decades.

In fact, even though BL lacked the real Sierra/Cavalier rival for another twelve months after the launch of the Maestro, and even though the latter made its branding, if anything, still more complex, the Maestro is by all accounts an excellent car – and BL had little trouble selling as many as it could make. The brand confusion (see Chapter 1) is merely another symptom (like the long and continuing lag in product line) of the huge catch-up that BL never quite completed. The improvement produced by just two properly researched, planned, and produced new models is evidence enough of the damage done by unplanned and incoherent reaction in the past.

But there is also, from the company, alas, damning evidence of a different kind. The Land Rover, one of the most successful models ever to emerge from a British car factory, was also one of the rare examples of a high-quality product good enough and unique enough to create its own market. For decades the Land Rover had that market virtually to itself, but by 1983 the situation for the product had changed out of all recognition.

It was then given its first major revamp in thirty-five years. Why? Because the four-wheel pioneer had been run a trifle ragged by competition from the Japanese, exploiting weaknesses that you would only expect from a product launched in 1948. Yet even that isn't the greatest tragedy. To quote the *Financial Times*: 'Land Rover has still to tap the potential in North America where, until now, it has not sold any of its products.' That's less an opportunity than an indictment.

Second-Best Is Worse

In both its marketing and its product strategy, the Rover management (and its masters at BL) had made the fatal and fundamental error of forgetting that markets which are ignored are markets which are lost – either now or later. It wasn't the quality of the product that let the Land Rover down, but the quality of the marketing. That truth flies in the face of the new conventional wisdom about quality. For example, in 1984, a survey by market researchers KAE, *New Products in Groceries*, portrayed a great shift in attitudes among the surveyed grocers, who gave their main reasons for the success of the hits and, likewise, the failure of the also-limped. The new champ was 'good-excellent product quality' as opposed to the old winner, 'consumer demand/satisfaction'.

Now, at IBM, which knows whereof it speaks in these matters, quality is actually defined as meeting customer requirements in full. If the argument is that computers, even personal ones, obey different criteria from groceries, that still leaves a big question: what use is a high-quality product for which there is no consumer demand? Clearly quality, though (again) the *sine qua non*, was not the factor that propelled the top grocery launches of the past two years. The positive marketing value of quality can only come into play (and powerful play at that) where other offerings are perceived as inferior.

In the grocery trade, that play is far more difficult to achieve than in durable goods. There the problem is often negative quality; poor

Lancia took a long time to dispel the idea that its cars rust in the first rainfall; while Ford in the US has emphasized quality in its ads, not to jump ahead of the Japanese, but to stress that it no longer lags behind. As IBM's John R. Opel has pointed out to his troops, if their quality isn't good enough, customers will buy where it's better.

Yet the KAE quality findings are too conspicuous to be ignored. In 1980 quality got 62 per cent in the 'main reasons for success' score. It had climbed to 76 per cent in 1984 – heading towards double the downgraded figure for consumer demand/satisfaction. Perhaps these numbers should be treated with a pinch of packaged salt: do the surveyed grocers really believe that distinct product advantage, competitive price and continued advertising support are significantly less important success factors than quality?

If so, they are wrong. The positioning of a product in the market, both in differentiation and price, is what determines success – and you won't get that without strong and continuous advertising, either. That, of course, is elementary. What the grocers were really doing was catching the spirit of the times: in saturated, highly competitive markets, consumers with large spending power will not be fobbed off with second-best. For new products, which have other steep hills to climb, second-best is the surest route to dying in the cold. But that means second-best, not just in quality, but in everything else in the mix of marketing.

5: He Who Levitates Is Lost

All markets are finite, even for the fortunate firm that has achieved transcendent superiority in perceived value. Sooner or later dynamic growth comes to an end, replacement sales come to dominate demand and, depending on the degree of competition, profitability comes under pressure ranging from the excruciating to the infuriating. These days fate may pass its stern decree even with an innovation – maybe especially with one, if Konosuke Matsushita, that greatest of Japanese corporate architects, is to be believed.

In the eighties (his own and the century's), Matsushita said this: 'An innovation ought to be good for two or three years: today, the same day you put a new product on the market, it's out-of-date. We are so over-eager to compete that we spoil a new product by coming out with an even newer one.' That true observation raises a cruel paradox for anybody who (rightly) urges Western industry to innovate with new products and processes and to invest in the very latest equipment as the only way to combat the fiendish Orientals and to stay viable in the *macho* competitive markets that lie ahead.

What's the use, after all, if the result is merely to innovate the product, and maybe the whole company, into obsolescence? The experience of a company called Agemaspark is enough to chill the innovative body to the marrow. Agemaspark had to call in the receivers, even though its baubles – electro-discharge spark eroders – were in the front line of machine shop technology, sold well enough abroad to earn a Queen's Award, and promised well enough to attract £2 million of public money.

The basic trouble with the eroders, though, was erosion of their market. Turnover all but halved between 1979 and 1981, making it

78

small wonder that the loss rose to 56 per cent of sales. High technology is not, like virtue, its own reward – and the company's marketing base (let alone its financial one) was simply too narrow to survive recession and also support development.

In other words innovations, like anything else in marketing, have to pass stiff tests of viability before they justify commitment of funds. The same can be true even of internal innovations, which won't be directly damaged by adverse competition or market conditions – but will be indirectly involved up to the neck. Take the case of BL's Longbridge plant, which in the spring of 1982 had to make a further cutback of 500 in the labour force producing the Metro. The necessity was attributed to 'over-production' – another word for Agemaspark's problem of under-selling.

Emulating the robotic brooms of the Sorcerer's Apprentice, the highly automated Metro line had simply been churning out more cars than the market could take. This neatly gives the lie to the received rubbish that British industry's problems all stem from under-supply of products which, if only the tap were turned higher, would be lapped up. The reality was usually that, even if the factories had produced at capacity, the same inferior management that was ultimately responsible for the low production and poor productivity would also have ensured that mistakes in product design and marketing imposed just as formidable a roadblock.

At the time of its Sorcerer's Apprentice problems, the Metro, for all the ballyhoo of its beginnings, had settled down as a reasonable, but not a resounding success: a first-quarter UK market share of 6½ per cent compared with the Ford Escort's 11 per cent, while the new Metro variants on the way were bound to run into even more intense competition. But none of this meant that BL was wrong to launch the Metro, or wrong to invest so heavily in automated production. On the contrary, the received view is perfectly justified – without those innovations in product and production, BL's plight would obviously have been far more parlous. Its tragedy is that costs of investment have had to be spread over too low a mass-market volume, because of the general erosion of its one-time market strengths.

The erosions of Agemaspark, while very different in origin, have a similar explanation. The high-tech niche really is the right target for a skilled engineering firm. But the high status of its technology won't spare it from the low-down viability tests of low-tech marketing. It has to be the right firm with the right product at the right time – a truism which only becomes an insight because so many companies ignore its self-evident prescriptions.

Agemaspark couldn't adjust to shifts in the market because it only had the one highly specific product: BL couldn't, either, because its Metro line could only produce one highly specific car. Flexibility is the key to adaptability, and the latter is what opens the door to the highest profits in markets which are changing, in tastes and technology, so rapidly as today's. Yet despite these absolute imperatives of the market, many companies go down for the third time by failing to observe the truths of that tune-calling market.

Toying with the Company

Take the British toy industry. Were not its calamities so universal that no individual managers could fairly be given the blame? Anybody looking from afar at the fatalities in the British toy industry would obviously be inclined to exculpate the managements concerned – how could it be all their fault? First Dunbee-Combex-Marx, then Airfix, then Lesney: the line, when you include the lesser extinguished lights, is nastily long. But closer examination shows the Big Three to be catastrophes of such different orders that the turmoil in toys can only be one factor, although a most weighty one, contributing to their downfalls.

The effect of the market slump should not, in fact, be exaggerated. Managements customarily preen themselves, and expect to be preened by others, when riding an irresistible boom. By the same token they must expect, and deserve, the blame when their market turns nasty on them. What happens, sadly more often than not, is that riding high literally takes managers' feet off the ground. That's when they gallop full speed ahead into ambitious projects which only seem splendid in the light of those dazzling boom-time profits. For instance, one of the former DCM twins, Richard Beecham and Basil Feldman, used to boast about all the wonders which English management had demonstrated to the incompetent US toy industry; but it was their American failure which brought the pair tumbling down.

The wise marketer never forgets that America is the toughest competitive nut: you may crack it this year, only to find that today's triumph is tomorrow's disaster. In the toy market, however, this is a general, not a specifically American truth. Toys are a fashion industry. In fickle markets like these, guessing right consistently is well nigh impossible. The marketer must either take the fashion element out of his product range (no easy trick), or diversify away from fickle fashions, or maintain great fleetness of foot.

Implementation of the first and third strategies can be achieved. For example the Quaker Oats subsidy, Fisher-Price, in America, the Lego business in Europe, and even the little old English toy soldier firm of Britain's have soldiered on through tough trading conditions by creating indispensable ranges with a secure niche in long-running markets, and by constantly adding products to the range – often by exemplary innovation – to catch the latest toy trends.

Do that, and you continue to exercise a firm hold on the trade. It appears in retrospect that the basic Airfix range – model kits – didn't have enough exclusive strength to serve as a support in times of trouble as well as glory. A policy of diversifying away from toys, into supplying Marks & Spencer with shoes, for example, made at least superficial sense. But that couldn't be said of the decision to buy Meccano from the long-running Lines disaster. The Meccano set had long been dislodged from its prime position in children's hearts and retailers' shelves.

Airfix was merely doubling its pain. The writing duly appeared on its wall as long ago as March 1978, when its bank debt stood at all but three times the level of a year before; the next year it nearly doubled, and then did so again. The saga of Lesney, a much larger firm which also never got far enough away from its toy base, outshines (or outshadows) even that: 4,8,23,46 (against turnover of 107) – so reads the four-year run, in round millions of pounds, of its total bank indebtedness. If only its customers had been as enthusiastic as its bankers. On figures like these, one harsh conclusion is inescapable: sure, the markets failed the firms, but so did the managements.

Like DCM, Lesney was originally seduced by its own super-growth; then, doubly seduced by its triumphant comeback from a previous market disaster, it advanced boldly from recovery into its final, fatal, phase. The die-cast model car market hasn't proved capable of providing the secure, expandable base for successful extension of a Lego. Lesney found itself making a commodity product in a fashion market: a deadly combination. Its original near-Nemesis in cars, Hot Wheels, came from Mattel, which next, faced with and financially tortured by the same problem as above, branched out into electronic toys.

Video games took Mattel into personal computers, and computers into what was to become the most violently buffeted market of them all: one in which a levitated toy firm was perhaps the least likely competitor. In any event, Mattel sank into massive losses as its new market's boundaries hemmed in the company in their turn. Mattel had bounded out of the low-tech frying pan into the high-technology fire.

Shoot the Pianist

Again, the temptation is to blame the market, not the management – an interesting reversal of theory, which holds that failure has few friends, in management as in anything else. In practice, though, the failed business can attract as much sympathy and attempted succour as the victim of a traffic accident. But a business collapse like Mattel's is seldom accidental – somebody (or some bodies) made awful mistakes. On that truth, one John M. Langham is a priceless example, priceless because what marks him out from fellow managers is the rank heresy of actually confessing to his failure: 'I am certainly prepared to take my share of the blame as a member of the board.'

The board in question was that of Stone-Platt, from which Langham bought the ships' propeller business after fourteen years running one of the divisions. The heretic, writing to the *Financial Times*, made the following incontrovertible points:

1. The merger between Stone (engineering) and Platt (textile machinery) had no logic in the marketplace or anywhere else.

2. Their union merely kept in being businesses that should have been closed, and did so at the expense of better businesses.

3. The once-successful Platt speciality in textiles performed badly after the merger for reasons within management's control.

4. The board (this is where Langham shoulders his share of the blame) failed to provide 'effective direction' or 'to take the difficult decisions'.

Failure of this nature deserves its lack of friends; and, as Langham argues very forcefully, the collapse of Stone-Platt when the Midland Bank pulled the plug was a failure of the management, not of the bank or 'the system', as some fond fellows have prattled. Of course, it's fair to feel sympathy for the last chairman, who arrived on the doomed ship too late. It had been doomed because, rather than develop what they had, in markets which would have tested the strength and ingenuity of greater men, the two sides acted as if, by joining, their respective problems had somehow been solved. In fact, amalgamations only solve competitive problems if they remove the competition from the market, or draw its sting by extracting its strengths. Even then, in modern conditions, the respite may be only temporary: the larger competitive target created by the amalgamation may attract sharper and more devastating shooters.

No known circumstances can eliminate the need for meticulous attention to markets and their demands, or for continuous re-orientation of the company to align it with the market now and with the trends of its future development. If the finite market is too small to support the company, as Lesney's and Agemaspark's become too small, the company must either make a sideways jump into new, sustaining, and substantial areas, or else it must go under. As Langham, formerly of Stone-Platt, says, 'Terminating organizations and managements which are no longer successful for whatever reason, and regenerating new ones to take over' is the lifeblood of a successful economy. But it is far better for the economy, and for the unfortunate employees who get trapped by failure, if regeneration takes place within the firm – and that demands outwitting the always finite markets, as opposed to over-rating them.

Heller's Golden Rules

HOW TO . . .

. . . KEEP IN TOUCH
1: Let young people make the running
2: Give market decisions to people who live from and off the market
3: Use continuous, organized questioning and questing to get variants and variations

. . . CONTROL BIGNESS
1: Make the whole worth more than its good parts – by building the latter
2: Match new markets to new management styles
3: Make subsidiaries responsible for strategies as well as tactics

83

. . . BUILD BUSINESS
1: Follow the laws of Scad: segment, concentrate and develop
2: Increase market concentration by broadening market coverage
3: Change distribution methods to match changing markets

. . . IMPROVE PROFIT QUALITY
1: Translate perceived value into price related to volume – and thus to costs
2: Make product planning the foundation of market planning
3: Shun second-best in anything unless you *want* to be an also-ran

. . . DODGE DIFFICULTY
1: Don't just be the firm with the right product; be the right firm with the right product at the right time
2: If you fail your markets, don't blame it on them
3: Cut what doesn't work – and reinforce what does

SECTION THREE
ECONOMICS

1: The No-Way No-Hope No-Win

If you sincerely want to be poor, enter with a product that hasn't a chance in a market where you haven't a hope. To achieve this non-achievement, all managers need do is form a wholly erroneous set of views about their product, their competitors, their market, and their talents. To raise the art to its highest pitch, however, the project must also involve such awesome costs that failure will bankrupt the company.

That makes aerospace companies prime candidates for non-success with no-hope projects. The expenditure is so gigantic, the economics so finely balanced, and the market so furiously competitive that nobody in full possession of their natural senses, you might suppose, would ever seek to break in from scratch. Yet Lockheed did so with the TriStar, whose shut-down in 1981 cost it a $400 million write-off – but this was only part of the pain inflicted by this ill-starred attempt of a military contractor to break into civil aviation. Since 1972 the plane had cost $1 billion; it hadn't even covered its start-up costs in all that time. Worse, this was Lockheed's second disastrous bite at the civil cherry: it had earlier lost a fortune on the Electra turbo-prop in much the same way.

Just why Lockheed failed to learn its Electra lesson illustrates the dangers of too much corporate strategy. Dependence on any one market, or any one customer, naturally worries any company; if customer and market are the same (the US military in Lockheed's case), the perfect strategy surely demands a major diversified market somewhere else. Equally, sound strategy uses a company's existing strong suits – and Lockheed was brilliant at designing and building military aircraft. It wasn't, judging by the Electra, much good at marketing civil ones: but nobody's perfect.

86

Unfortunately, if not perfect, Douglas is highly proficient at marketing airliners, and clobbered Lockheed heavily with the DC10. Thus Lockheed did not repeat its Marketing Error One (coming in much too late – the Electra arrived just in time to be comprehensively leapfrogged by the pure jet). Instead, it committed Marketing Error Two – plunging into a two-horse race with prizes only enough for one; and where the winner will not, by any stretch of the imagination, be you.

It's rare that a critical writer on such affairs can deny the charge of hindsight. But long, long ago, before the traumas of the Rolls-Royce bankruptcy and allied RB-211 troubles, long before TriStar drove Lockheed itself to the financial brink, I observed that this second attempt to crack the civil market was gravely over-stretching the Lockheed finances; was over-reliant on a financially unreliable engine supplier; and was dependent on selling at least 300 planes – a total nowhere in sight, certainly not within an economic timespan. Actually, Lockheed never made the magic 300. As the blade of the guillotine fell, some 230–40 TriStars were in service or on order with airlines – after a decade of hard work (not to mention the odd enormous bribe).

It's ironic to recall how Rolls-Royce bust itself, metaphorically speaking, to get the order for TriStar engines, and then really did bust itself in the effort to supply them. The orders added up to some 750 engines, which sounds great, until one fact is called to mind. As the *Financial Times* delicately put it, 'It is thought unlikely that much if any of the RB-211 work for the TriStar programme has been carried out at substantial profits.' The TriStar was a born loser for everybody involved, except those lucky sub-contractors who were paid at profitable prices for their contribution to an unprofitable certainty.

Fairness demands noting that sometimes market forces do drive managements into projects which, left peacefully to themselves, they would have shunned. The chemical giants, for instance, have often faced the dilemma of knowing that too much capacity by far is being installed, but of knowing also that, unless they add to the excess themselves, they will inevitably lose market share, and maybe their whole market. The correct answer, of course, is to accept that unpleasant consequence rather than be dragged down (like the aforesaid giants) into permanent over-capacity and price depression. The answer is very difficult to accept. If it's refused, though, the difficulties are far greater.

The Low-Return Leaders

In any case, the pursuit or defence of market share can be a snare and a delusion – according to an article in the *Harvard Business Review*. Its findings go right against the entrepreneurial grain, for every entrepreneur loves the thought of cornering the largest share of the market, and with it (naturally) the most in profits, prestige and price. Well, nature doesn't necessarily imitate art. To take one example, in rental cars, Hertz has constantly suffered from intense price and non-price competition offered by the also-rans: indeed, from 1978 to 1982, Budget (ranking fourth) pushed up earnings by 27%, while Hertz's profits declined by a total of $110 million.

Then there's American Can, and Georgia Pacific, and Goodyear – all companies which have produced lower returns than smaller competitors. As the article comments: 'Despite the usually strong correlation between market share and profitability, clearly the benefits of dominance are not universally enjoyed.' Does the explanation lie in rotten management or rotten markets?

The article's author, Carolyn Y. Woo, has studied 112 examples of market leaders with low returns – and has found the reasons why they have them. Such companies tend to operate in regional or fragmented markets (where there are more than twenty competitors). A regional basis, she says, may not yield many cost advantages over competitors. In fragmented markets, too, the many competitors indicate that there are low entry barriers – as well as product and process characteristics which favour a range of skills and sizes, and not just one monolithic supplier.

Unstable market environments are also unpromising – meaning those where businesses have more frequent product and technological changes, but where these frequent changes don't boost demand. Instead, the chopping and changing merely intensify the competition for existing volume. Then, watch out for markets where conditions are deteriorating: i.e. more firms are quitting the market than joining. Businesses with low value-added are also vulnerable: they are sensitive to suppliers' cost increases, but have less chance of passing them on to customers. In markets where customer service and professional support are very important, the expenses of leadership can be especially severe: while in markets for capital goods and (less often) those connected with materials and components, it can be unprofitable to lead.

In fact, though, it turns out to be weaknesses of the companies rather than their markets that are the key to feeble performance. Woo notes that the low-return leaders tended to have a worse reputation for quality (defined as the difference between the percentage of products judged superior to competitors' and the percentage of products judged inferior). The quality levels for low- and high-return market leaders were 31% and 48% respectively. Low-return leaders tended to charge higher prices and also shouldered heavier costs than their competitors, while (in percentage terms) spending on their product R&D wasn't much greater, on process R&D it was actually lower. They made less active selling and advertising efforts too. 'Overall, the findings reinforce the conclusion that the competitive posture of the low-return market leaders was inconsistent and did not match their market and product characteristics well': i.e., they were badly managed.

There's one final, very significant point. The low-return leaders tended to share more marketing resources between different parts of the business. Some 51% of the low-return group shared more than four-fifths of the marketing programmes with other lines of business, compared with only 39% of the high-return leaders; and 66% of the low-return group shared more than one-quarter of the marketing channels, as against 58% for the high returns.

Successful marketing companies these days give carefully defined separate businesses their own distinct marketing resources – meaning the resources they need to sell effectively. It's the unsuccessful business which muddles up the marketing. In other words, the no-way no-hope no-win condition isn't generally inescapable or irreparable for the low-return leaders. They can win, if they want to. It isn't as if, for example, they were shelling out millions for something they didn't understand, whose future was wholly unpredictable, and which didn't exist elsewhere in any profitable shape or form.

Nimslo's Bedraggled Canary

Would anybody? They certainly would. If capitalism, as its opponents allege, is on its last legs, it's certainly been showing some amazing turns of speed of precisely this type. There was a time when products actually had to reach the market before the proud possessors made their mints – and even then years of waiting were generally required. Now the shrewd cookie can rake in real negotiable cash before a single member of the paying public has laid hands on the product.

That was merely one twist in the extraordinary Nimslo 3D saga. By selling all his shares before a London placing which attempted to value this company (whose 3D camera hadn't earned a bean at that date) at £230 million, inventor Jerry Nims cleared, according to report, at least £4 million. Here beginneth the mystery – not why anyone in their right mind would pay that kind of money for several million birds in the bush, but why Nims tried to jump off the bandwagon so soon (as an investor: he still took a $150,000 salary as chief executive).

After all, Nimslo's forecasts had been going up by leaps and bounds. By Year Four of actual trading (1985), sales were supposed to hit $735 million and profits $156 million. Believe it or not (and anybody could be forgiven if they didn't), that was *half* the current sales of Polaroid, which was much nearer Year Forty than Year Four. As chief executive, Nims must obviously have authored the forecasts: translate them into share price terms, and his £4 million bird in the hand began to look like a distinctly bedraggled canary.

Indeed, the history of great marketing entrepreneurs, including Polaroid's Dr Edwin Land, has mostly been marked by a reluctance to part with even a tithe of their estate, beside which Custer's Last Stand, Horatio's resistance on the Tiber bridge and the Trojan clinging to Helen were but feeble gestures. Your true marketing genius, convinced that, say, 3D cameras will sweep the world, identifies with the wonder so totally that he can't bear the thought of any separation – especially if the part being separated is his wallet. Indeed, that identification is one of his sustaining and driving forces: and persistence and drive are the crucial ingredients of marketing success.

No doubt it was the fact that some such dark thoughts were running through investors' minds that next persuaded Nims to reinvest in his company. It can't have been an improvement in the trading position, because the truth was beginning to dawn that the Nimslo camera was over-priced, very hard to market and moving very slowly – even at the sharply cut price which was forced on the management. To achieve stunning triumph, Nimslo only had to do a quarter as well at selling cameras as in selling equity to the City of London: but that was a terribly tall order; and sure enough in 1983, Nimslo brilliantly succeeded in losing $10.6 million *more* than its $26.2 million turnover.

The key to such sagas is that terribly tall stories have become much easier to believe in an age of technological miracles, when mysterious products make magical millions for unknown entrepreneurs, based on solid market success. The existence of these everyday miracles makes it more, not less, important to ask the economic questions and do the economic sums. It may still be necessary to take a leap in the dark. But the wise marketer first does all in his power in the daytime to check where the obstacles are placed – and the exact position of the door marked 'Exit'.

2: The Cost–Output–Sales Factor

The Nimslo saga introduces a new wrinkle into one of the oldest marketing games of all – determining how much sales will rise if the price is cut, and whether the additional turnover thus achieved will yield more profit. In Nimslo's case, the rate of sales at the original, excessive, price was so low that the question never had to be asked: no price cut, no sales.

In companies which are in a happier position, the equation turns partly on the extent to which higher volume generates lower unit costs. One of Henry Ford's most brilliant business breakthroughs was his exploitation of the fact that lower prices not only greatly expanded volume (so that, other things being equal, profits would have been higher by the amount of the extra sales), but that other things were not equal. As volume rose, so unit costs, both fixed and variable, declined by more than the cuts in price.

That's why entrepreneurs down the ages have generally sought to maximize volume rather than price. Occasionally the policy has led to disaster – for example, at Texas Instruments, where what worked wonders in semi-conductors flopped, not only in watches, but also in home computers. In TI's base of micro-electronics, the decline in prices as volume increased wasn't optional – it was an inevitable consequence of the technology and the market. In the consumer areas where TI tried its luck, a low-price policy merely took the company away from the zone of premium quality and technological superiority which was its natural positioning.

In other misled companies, the great marketing myth is that the rate of production determines not so much their profit as their level of sales. That is, the only determinant of turnover is the amount which they are able to produce. Now, there are indeed companies whose policy is always to expand supply by rather less than the rise in demand: Waterford Glass and Mercedes-Benz are examples from very different fields. It's a difficult feat of balance, but one which is never demanded of the mass producers.

You wouldn't think so to hear them talk, however. To a car company, output lost through a strike equates with lost turnover – although in nearly all cases the 'losses' in sales are made up after the resumption of output. The same fallacy leads producers to say, when in possession of unfilled orders, 'We could have sold more, if only we could have made more.' Maybe they could, and maybe they couldn't. The market, and only the market, determines true sales potential, and that can only be tested in conditions of full supply.

In an industry like British cars, long troubled by disruptive labour disputes and production snarl-ups, the myth took hold with particular ease. The real question was whether the factories concerned could make at low enough cost sufficiently attractive models to win a large and growing share of the world market. The question was begged by much of the comment which attended the obsequies as the British car industry shrank slowly in the West, led downwards by its former flagship, BL.

Where Rover Strayed

When sentence of death was passed in 1981 on Rover's £31 million Solihull factory, opened just five years before, one account of that unavailing struggle called the works 'The showpiece plant that never stood a chance'. The *Sunday Times* report underneath that headline gave some harsh supporting facts. Planned to produce the current range of Rover saloons, the plant had a top capacity of 3,000 vehicles a week and a break-even of 2,000. Output never got much above half capacity – despite the fact that (*sic*) 'The old Rover factory had always sold more cars than they could make.' That clever trick goes to the core of the problem, for it is, of course, impossible to sell what you can't make. What the writer meant was that Rover never managed to satisfy the latent demand for its cars.

This deficiency was especially serious at the time of the launch – always a tough period for manufacturers, who must smoothly phase out the old and phase in the new, in factory and marketplace, without causing undue problems in either location. That's a tricky procedure. When launching the Sierra, Ford was hindered, for example, by an excessive overhang of the previous Cortina models. But in Rover's case the launch of its new range was ruined at factory level – by shortage of supply. For a full year, weekly output ran at a pitiful 500 or 600 cars. Any marketing impetus achieved by an excellent design (Car of the Year in 1976) was dissipated by too little of two essentials – availability and reliability. By the time that reasonable rates of output had been achieved, UK car sales were suffering generally (especially those of larger cars). But it's no use blaming the fuel crisis – the relative and remarkable stability and success of Mercedes and BMW in the years of Rover's decline give the lie to that particular excuse.

The necessity of achieving high stocks and a rapid build-up to planned output levels in a launch period mustn't be confused with the creation and satisfying of long-term demand. Probably every successful launch runs into supply shortages: these certainly afflicted IBM's runaway Personal Computer. But Rover's problem was one of inefficiency rather than insufficiency. The bungled production of the launch year was only one aspect of the blunders which botched Rover's otherwise laudable effort to break into the bigger time. Other errors included:

1. Late pre-production changes in the detail design by non-Rover people from BL, which spoilt the ship, and not even for a ha'p'orth of tar.

2. Central veto of various models with which Rover could have built on the original launch – and taken up spare capacity.

3. The limitations imposed by enforced use of a body plant elsewhere in BL.

4. The failure to build up an overseas franchise of any significance.

Of course, shortage of supplies would have been fatal to export sales, even if the BL marketing organization had done its job properly in America and other overseas markets (which it didn't).

Lest it be concluded that this justifies the observation about 'selling more cars than we could make', bear in mind that the preconditions of selling anything at all, especially in an overseas market, include getting adequate stock into the showrooms and the back-up areas. If that supply is lacking, it's a question of not being able to sell cars (or anything else), period. While ultimately it's always demand that

94

creates supply, supply has a prime function in ensuring that demand can exist at all.

In sum, then, factors arising from the BL merger helped to prevent the Rover company from developing along the lines of its internal logic as an integrated producer of a range of quality executive cars. Production failings then ensured that Rover couldn't overcome the inherent drawbacks. The case never became a question of selling more cars than they could make, but one of making fewer cars than they could sell – until they could sell so few that, agonizingly, the problem cured itself.

That very often does happen to companies which diagnose their problems as being 'oversold'. By the time that condition is cured, managements are apt to find themselves in the far worse situation of over-producing. But this has very seldom been the case with British car companies (and not just BL). The harsh truth – that often they could not actually have sold the cars of which their marketers were deprived by the action or inaction of blue-collar employees – is the same verity which gives the lie to another endearing notion: that putting all the jobless back to work would inflate the British gross domestic product by an easily worked out equation. That would only be true if markets could be found for all the products that would, in theory, pour forth. In the 1973–83 period, a time when manufacturing industry was mostly having quite enough trouble, in practice, selling what it actually *could* supply, that weird economic theory wasn't even remotely tenable.

The Coal Mountain

The economic truth can be seen with stark clarity from the experience of the National Coal Board, which demonstrates that, while the link between productivity and marketing isn't one of the best explored aspects of management, it is decisive. The NCB has been compelled to grasp the marketing reality: that there's no point in pressing people to buy your wonder-product if you simply can't deliver the goods. The pay carrots dangled in front of its face-workers to make them mine more coal, and the hard marketing sell presented to industrial users to make them buy that coal, were two sides of the same coin. Popping the coin in the slot, however, landed the Board with two crises at once: the biggest stocks and strikes in its history: although the protested pit closures were made inevitable by the coal mountain.

Criticism of the Board for conjuring up its own calamity is unfair, in one respect. In coal, as in many other industries, production planning is essentially (and very) long-term, while the recession which crunched energy consumption was essentially short-term (although on the long side of short, alas). But that common reaction in companies high and low, to equate production shortfalls with lost sales, when the two phenomena are quite plainly not the same thing at all, could hardly be disproved more dramatically.

There are only three possible solutions (which can be combined and permed) to an NCB-style mountain:

1. Slash prices until the mountain moves.
2. Keep on piling.
3. Cut production and/or capacity to bring supply and demand into balance.

The first is no good if you go bankrupt. The second, whoever finances it, prolongs the bad times at the expense of the good (stockpiling machine tools with public finance helped to kill the fine old machine tool firm of Alfred Herbert). The third, cutting capacity, is what the NCB is seeking to do. The strikers urging it to retain the old uneconomic pits didn't seem to understand that their survival can only be at the expense of the new, highly economic and enormously costly facilities which are the industry's rightful pride and joy. Sacrificing the new to the old is what happened at British Steel – with predictably dreadful results.

There is, of course, a fourth alternative: to stimulate demand so that it soaks up the super-abundant supply. But the Coal Board had no means this side of heaven of achieving that result. Nor did the chemical companies which found themselves in so severe a plight in the 1970s that, as one executive complained at the time, 'The only way I can affect the level of business is to insult one of my customers.'

The sovereign power of the market is something that even the firm which genuinely could sell more than it can make must watch and respect at all times. The market has a nasty habit of reasserting itself when least expected – and what makes Mercedes-Benz so strong is its faithful, unremitting observation and service of the market that it always *slightly* under-supplies. That's the key: let 'slightly' become severely, and the seller's market will one day vanish away – and not so softly and silently, either.

3: The Unkindest Cuts of All

One supreme fact tells more about the market position of a product, service, or company than any other: price – or, to be exact, relative price. Not only does price (obviously) determine one crucial dimension of profit: it also usually marks out the leader from the pack, and (which the leader may well not realize) establishes the degree of his vulnerability. That hidden weakness was laid hideously bare in recession when, one by one, the lordly names of the American market were falling from grace – sometimes after decades of uninterrupted financial beauty. Even Eastman Kodak slid down the hill which took heroes like Caterpillar tractors into actual and heavy loss. Kodak's 48 per cent fall in 1983 earnings, in terms of its own past record, was near disaster.

The causes were partly outside its control: the rise in the price of an essential raw material, silver, the soaring dollar, and the lingering impact of recession on Kodak's non-photographic sales. But beyond these transient factors lies the same long-term problem that reduced Caterpillar to a financial crawl and which has made dominant price leadership a thing of many pasts. The market from which Kodak gleaned such a rich harvest down the decades has become very mature. Even though Kodak's innovative thrust puts many another giant to shame, its excellent new products (the disc camera and super-fast colour film) are likely, at best, to defend its share of that over-ripe (i.e. slow-growing) market.

The difficulty is inevitable when you have as much as 85 per cent of the market at home, and half of all sales abroad. These are Kodak's figures for film, and from such dominant shares there's usually no way upwards. Even IBM, before the advent of its Personal Computer, had dropped from 60 per cent of the total computer market to 40 per cent. In the past, the few film competitors were too feeble technologically and in their marketing to capitalize on Kodak's strength, so to speak. But the Japanese are anything but feeble; Fuji has used the tried and true national recipe of making an equally good product at the lower costs which enable the market outsider to undercut a high-margin champion.

Like Caterpillar, the photo titan has always exploited its market strength to get the greatest prices and the most glorious margins (16.2 per cent back in 1973). Like the earth-moving giant, too, Kodak has been slow to move into new segments which are a long way from maturity. It does have a fast-growing business in copiers, true; but that market is now showing signs of congestion, and its leaders (including Xerox, another earlier victim of the Kodak virus) are moving as fast as their feet, and their feats, can carry them into the office of the future.

But the remarkable new phenomenon is that even the future's front line offers no protection. One widespread and unforeseen side-effect of the microelectronics revolution has been to create so great a product proliferation as to destroy price levels, make competition a nightmare, and utterly bewilder the consumer. Since using the personal computer itself can be bewildering for the purchaser, the result is one of the strangest boom markets in history. All over the world, people have been buying sophisticated machines in very large quantities and often at quite stiff prices; even at the lower end of the market, after a £116 cut, the Commodore 64 still cost £229. Because of the attractive potential of the market and the ease of design, manufacture, and entry created by the chip, it became almost anybody's game – or was, before IBM's success changed the rules.

So sweeping a spate of introductions and innovations simply gives the consumer too much choice. The consequences are inevitable. The price wars that forced down Sinclair's bottom-of-the-range machine to $29 in the United States will become endemic in many other product markets. The office of the future is likely to be hit by price wars even before that future has become reality. The pace will plainly become too hot for some. Already, as noted earlier, Texas Instruments' huge home computer losses have driven it from that market altogether, while Timex (which makes Sinclair's computers and used to market them in the States) has also quit the game.

Truth has become as strange as fiction in this process. In 1967, when

Ivor Williams began his *Management Today* series on a mythical company called Minipute, he thought up an obviously mythical product: the expendable computer. At $29, his dream has practically come true. The only trouble is that it probably means many expendable companies. The moral of these extraordinary goings–on will apply to many other sectors where the same technology-led market forces are at work. Prices will be stable for only a short time. Then the tumbling will begin – and the market leader won't be able to resist by virtue of his perceived pre-eminence. He will have to win through at the other end of the economic spectrum – cost.

High Margins and Low Costs

The argument was dramatized by General Motors when it tried in early 1982 to push through a deal cutting both its wages and its prices at a single stroke – to the great joy, no doubt, of its recession-hit salesmen. The salesman's prime article of faith, from highest to lowest, is that price is the prime selling weapon – and the lower the better. Give a salesman an inch in price, and he'll take a mile: which is why generations of marketing men have fought uphill to put across the (true) concept that profit or contribution, not volume, is the name of the game.

Of course, the twain are indissolubly linked, especially in a business like GM's in which a low volume of output has horrifying effects on huge manufacturing plants, especially if they have recently absorbed billions in capital spending. The catch, as many a marketing company has found in recession, is that a cut in prices unsupported by reductions in cost seldom generates enough volume to pay for the price damage. Hence GM's desire to persuade its car workers that $20 an hour, or $8 more than their beloved Japanese friends (or enemies), was too high a reward.

It's the reverse of what old Henry Ford did in a famous foray into economic theory. He *raised* pay to an unheard-of $5 an hour, reasoning that the higher level of worker prosperity would raise car sales, which would increase volume, which would lower unit costs – despite the five bucks. That worked because labour costs as a proportion of added value (a concept unknown in Ford's time, but which existed all the same) were much lower in those days. In the eighties, at GM and many other companies, this vital ratio had risen so high that price cuts couldn't be accommodated without destroying added value altogether.

The lesson is to pursue efficiencies in operations that will relentlessly reduce costs, so that, whether prices are under external or voluntary pressure, the company can take price cuts without profit destruction. That's why IBM has been automating what were already highly efficient, modern plants: because price leadership in turbulent conditions must be backed by, indeed, must go hand-in-hand with, cost leadership. Production and marketing have become two sides of the same coin. High margins obtained by low costs are highly defensible. High margins obtained by high prices are highly dangerous.

The recent history of the airlines demonstrates the point. In truth, if an airline doesn't use price as a weapon, there's precious little else at its disposal: price apart, convenience of schedule is by far the most important factor in determining who flies whom. Thus, on the Scottish routes, British Midland Airways, operating from Gatwick, beat the BA Shuttle, operating from the more convenient Heathrow, by the simple device of offering more for significantly less. In contrast, what shattered the transatlantic air trade and its profits was the advent of competitors offering a little less for tremendously less. The eventual ruinous free-for-all was proof that sensible managers should always seek the middle ground between Extreme A, charging so much that they stifle the growth of traffic (as on the European routes), and Extreme Z, charging so little that they fill the planes at little profit or even large loss (no small feat on a jumbo).

On the gamut from A to Z lie endless permutations and combinations of fares and services. But the major airlines, when threatened by the Laker onslaught, didn't attempt sophisticated or even smart solutions. They licked Laker by pouring resources into defending market share, even unto the destruction of their own profits. The way to large airline profits is by intensive employment of a carefully selected fleet – as demonstrated by Cathay Pacific. Cathay will even fly 747s on routes which look lopsided for such huge planes: 'misusing aircraft intelligently' is what Cathay's Duncan Bluck calls it. In translation, that means minimizing overall system costs. Combine that with maximizing overall system revenue (not, be it noted, *prices*) and you will not only survive the inevitable Price Wars, but thrive through them.

The Dynamics of Price

The truth is obvious. Yet there are, in this day and age, a few companies which think that pricing policies are not important in their marketing, and, much more serious, there are plenty (34 per cent of firms selling capital goods, 18 per cent of those making components, and 21 per cent of those supplying materials) which think that pricing is only 'fairly important'. Only a minority of firms seem to agree that price is vital (as it is; utterly and undeniably so): the figures are 12 per cent in capital goods, 20 per cent in components, and 18 per cent in materials.

Considering that price not only provides the only common feature for all kinds of goods, is one of the major factors in the customer's mind, and is a key determinant of profit, that's truly a strange approach to the market. Because of all this, any good business thinks about its prices all the time. Yet 'Too many companies try and run their businesses on the basis of keeping prices stable. This is particularly true of small companies – it might even be one reason why they stay small. Prices need to be constantly examined: not changed all the time, but examined. Price is too important an issue to be left alone for long.'

So writes marketing expert John Winkler. But what sort of examination do prices require? The research quoted (from an industrial market research survey entitled *How Industry Prices*) also shows unbelievably, but truly, that 81 per cent of companies fix their prices, not after examination of any meaningful kind, but by 'cost-related systems', either adding a fixed percentage to cost or taking a fixed margin off selling price. What's more, two-thirds of companies only 'sometimes' or 'rarely' modify this cost-based approach by 'non-cost related factors'.

This is rightly called 'an appalling situation' by Winkler. 'A very substantial proportion of industrial companies are still living in the dark ages of the industrial revolution when all you had to do was produce the product and the world would demand it.' The attitude is especially hard to understand given a Winkler example: a £10 million business with direct costs (material, labour, and production) adding up to £6 million; fixed costs (overheads, distribution, and sales) coming to £3.5 million; leaving £500,000 in profit. If you increase the sales by 25 per cent and hold fixed costs steady, you double the profits.

But hold sales steady and lower £4 million of material costs by 12½ per cent, while keeping fixed costs steady, too, and again you'll double your profits to a million. But: *you can achieve exactly the same effect by better pricing.* 'Increase your average prices by 5 per cent (through a different product sales mix), holding sales volume level and all costs level', and the million-pound trick is done. Which is easier – raising sales by a quarter, cutting material costs by 12½ per cent, or getting an average 5 per cent more out of your prices? The answer is as obvious as the results of increasing sales by 25 per cent, while cutting material costs by 12½ per cent and getting that 5 per cent price uplift on top. The company gets a profit of £2.6 million – over five times what it used to achieve.

When using 'non–cost related' factors to set selling prices, companies apparently refer to competitors' prices more than they conduct market studies when trying to determine how much they can or should charge. That's an improvement – but doing the market studies is obviously better still. For one thing, the company might be in an industry where everybody is charging less than the traffic will bear.

Beyond that, writes Winkler, in his book *Pricing for Results,*

> All of these companies calculate their costs, but they do not let them rule their decision. If the costs come out too high to enable them to make a profit, then they either find a way of reducing their costs or they do not go ahead with the product. Consulting the sales force is a sure way to drive your selling prices towards the floor. Unless it is handled with great skill and the sales force is objective, then it will be the worst method of all.

Pricing is never a cut-and-dried affair, however. Far from it. The aim is 'flexibility, surprise and economy of effort'. In other words, pricing in the dynamic company is a dynamic process. But note that the companies in the survey were asked another highly relevant question. Did they ever try to find out how acceptable their prices were to customers before taking the final decision on price? Two-thirds replied that they didn't. That is the greatest pricing error of them all.

4: Big Daddy Is Bad for You

The damage done to companies by outside price-cutters is by no means the only possible form of uninvited destruction. The enemy may be half within: the parent, who owns, finances or otherwise ultimately controls the child. This isn't a matter of excessive control in itself: indeed, it's often better if the bonds are complete. Thus, at a time when takeover bids were falling fast and thick (often in the pejorative meaning of the latter word) on the London stock market, one mega-million deal at least made mighty sense – the absorption by the old-line conglomerate BET of the Rediffusion minority held by outsiders.

Quite apart from its other virtues, the total union of parent and child gave BET the chance to find that market identity, or identification with markets, which it had conspicuously lacked: an increasing handicap in these days. The problem is not simply that of managing diversity. Rather, the old imperatives of being in the right market with the right product at the right time have been intensified as markets have fragmented, and as the number of competitors, all jockeying for position, has increased. You can't any more stroll into high potential growth operations in a fit of absent-mindedness, as Rediffusion itself did in computers.

Back in the 1970s the board explicitly forbade ventures into commercial data processing, a minefield which did indeed feature many large, mangled corpses. This was tough on the ambitions of the subsidiary which dominates the world flight simulator market (it claims 80 per cent) and wanted to move its simulator computer into the nascent market for mini-computers. But none of the directors minded the subsidiary pushing ahead with data entry machines – because none of them actually knew it was the very same minefield.

That in turn led to the subsidiary's development of videotex or viewdata systems, competing in a market for which $2.6 billion of sales has been predicted in Western Europe alone. That remains to be seen. But plainly a company in Rediffusion's lines of business, from cable to colour TV, paging systems to pneumatic tubes, must maximize its electronic expertise – and must apply these skills in the new growth markets.

For Rediffusion to succeed, and thus to lift a lumbering BET's growth, it had to make an across-the-board advance into becoming a full electronics-based information supplier. One consequence, if that effort were to succeed, was that BET's odds and ends would look odder still. It certainly wouldn't have missed the profits from the bundle of ill-fitting businesses which included an 'others' category (a giveaway label) that lost £5.6 million on £12.6 million of turnover in 1981–2. Nothing would justify BET in a policy of – well, rediffusion. Indeed, the logic of its position is that the parent should now take its sense of direction from the child.

The direction, though, must stay with the parent. Everybody and every management needs an ultimate master to exact performance. Binding BET and Rediffusion had the potential to result in better performance from both. But there's one parent or semi-parent, which never completely shares the objectives of its semi-children – and the consequences are seldom acceptable. That parent is the state.

Government's unhelpful influence can be seen even in the occasionally more successful cases, such as the computer company, ICL. At all times, the Big Daddy of the state has been in ICL's background: providing money on some occasions, favoured orders on many others. All marketing involves structuring a company or a product line to meet the freely arising demands of those customers whose business is truly profitable. If you introduce non-market factors, like Big Daddy, that essential marketing structure may never fall into place.

Indeed, some American research seems to prove that when Big Daddy, no matter whether he's the state or some stupidly proud corporate parent, keeps an unviable operation alive only by massive infusions of money, the fractious child never, never comes to good. Time and again, no matter how many millions are lost, or how many crack captains are pressganged to man the sinking ship, sink it continues to do.

With no Big Daddy around, drastic private solutions may, or must, follow. But Papa's presence puts off that vital day of facing the market realities: in ICL's case, that meant the point of recognizing that a customer base weighted too heavily in the UK can't support across-the-board competition with IBM: and that ICL's across-the-board philosophy helped to make its marketing image fuzzy compared to the diamond-blue hardness of an IBM.

Marketing, not technology, is the ultimate key to computer riches. ICL has been squeezed between IBM's general market strength on one side, and the powerful specialized positions occupied in areas like small computers or banking or retailing by other US competitors. The new regime which took over in 1981 acted bravely to counter this situation by link-ups designed to fill the yawning gaps in its range, while striving to establish a clear, coherent identity – inside and outside the company – which is and should be forced on firms which must survive in markets on their merits, and which can never count on any Big Daddy's non-commercial blessing. To prove the point, merely compare these figures. Company A in four successive years made £153 million; £161 million; £225 million; £255 million. Company B earned £25 million; lost £50 million; earned £24 million; then £46 million. The first is IBM (UK): the second ICL.

Victor Kiam's Rich Shave

The Big Daddies capable of allowing such situations to develop and persist do not consist only of politicians and civil servants. Bankers can serve the same silly purpose. Take the collapse, previously mentioned, of the toy firm, Lesney. The very ability of a £100 million turnover like Lesney's to attract finance from foolish bankers itself contributes to the finality of disaster: merely prolonging the agony, while the afflicted firm runs further downhill into traumas (Lesney's were in production mishaps and overstocking).

In raw capitalist theory, a healthy economy needs bankruptcies as well as bonanzas. But too often a more tender approach prevails – that while there's life, there's not only hope, but a chance that the banks will recover their lost loot. It sometimes happens, too. But that depends on the existence of the very things that Lesney lacked: a strong market share in an attractive, well-defined niche. It's the exploitation of such positions which explains the embarrassing

105

examples of companies which, when prised loose from Big Daddy, proceed to perform wonders of growth.

That's what came to pass when Victor Kiam liked his Remington razor so much that he bought the company, lifting it off the giant Sperry conglomerate, which had lost $30 million on the subsidiary in the previous four years. Kiam proceeded to double both Remington's US market share and its total sales, which shot up to $150 million – on which the pre-tax profits came to $12 million. What had Kiam got, or done, that Big Daddy hadn't?

One unique thing he had, for certain, was independence: the purchaser was rich enough to put up a million of his own (vastly outweighed by bank indebtedness of $24 million – paid back, though, in twelve months) to buy the company. The second asset was speed of execution and decision – an immediate cost-cutting programme that cost 70 executives their jobs, and was linked with equally swift measures to improve quality. But the third asset was decisive – the marketing smarts that Kiam had learnt from his career with Lever Brothers.

Three marketing decisions were crucial. First, Kiam spoke to the retailers and found out why they wouldn't carry stocks – because of rapid product replacement by new versions. Kiam promptly slowed down the new product programme, thus also saving money. Second, he broadened the range by adding a new model aimed at a carefully chosen price point: $19.95. This was half the price of any other shaver on the market, and reaped a rich harvest from the gift customers – 500,000 units sold in the first year.

Third, Kiam kept up the advertising pressure in a highly intensive mode – even sacrificing profits to maintain a very heavy spend. All these actions had been available to Sperry. Its failure to take them sprung from orientation towards investment, as opposed to the all-marketing slant which Kiam brought to his task (and his vast personal profit). There's the vital difference. Little Daddy brings concentrated marketing smarts to bear. Big Daddy tries to make the investment pay off without understanding the market: and often ends up sending good millions after bad.

Viable Shares in Viable Markets

The explanation goes right to the core of why BET was absolutely correct in merging with its child, Rediffusion. Companies are only worth backing if they have, or can develop, viable shares in viable markets. The larger their losses, the greater their inability to finance themselves, the less likely it is that they possess viability either in present or future markets. The more competitive the world scene, the more vital it is that a company be built round its viable markets – and viability can never be achieved by producing some object which is not covering its true costs in the market, because part of those costs is being carried by somebody else outside the marketplace.

Moreover, since the fundamental deficiency lies in the overall stance in markets, it cannot be cured unless those financing the cure are deeply involved in these markets. Bankers and bureaucrats never are. In the excitement of the chase after jobs for workers or contracts for companies or a foothold in new technology, eyes are never on the ball or the goal – building a profitable long-term enterprise round its markets. Hence the chain of Pyrrhic victories in state-aided competition; the eventually catastrophic Rolls-Royce contract for the Lockheed TriStar engines, described in the first part of this section, and the crash of the De Lorean Dream (attracted to Belfast after vigorous competition between public authorities), are among the saddest examples.

Merely read the reports on the Crown Agents fiasco, in which £200 million of public money melted away, and you see how honest men and women in government allow public money to be devoured in deeply doubtful ventures: not because they are inattentive, but because they are attending to other things. Managers, however, have no excuse for directing their attention to matters other than building that profitable, lasting enterprise and properly executing all the accompanying short-term tasks. Anything else is a 'lapse' – the term which, judging by the Crown Agents' report, Whitehall uses for crass stupidity or misjudgement. No doubt, if anybody ever investigates the De Lorean episode in equal detail, the record will be littered with lapses and 'criticisms' (one rung down in the pecking or whipping order).

With equal certainty, the lapsed will produce countless excuses. The Reagan recession, and the loss of confidence caused by financial uncertainty when the UK government backers finally took fright, have already been thrust forward in De Lorean's self-defence. The jury will ignore these claims – and rightly. The whole Belfast project was predicated on sales that far exceeded any likely share of the US car market. That was a far greater weakness than trying to establish a greenfield mass manufacturing operation in Northern Ireland *per se*.

You can indeed start from scratch, with no labour force, no manufacturing tradition, no markets and no products – and win: in the green fields of Ireland, too. Waterford Glass did so long ago. But its founders built slow, learned the hard way (by observed experience), became ambitious with success (not before it), and didn't have a Big Daddy government in the wings, pouring out millions. Also, of course, they didn't have John Z. De Lorean.

5: Too Small Is Ugly

One of the massive forces stripping the naked market bare is the loss of the security that used to lie in economies of scale. This isn't because its components have disappeared: as ever, the learning curve still halves production costs with each cumulative doubling of output; as ever, the costs of marginal output diminish as production rises. But fast-changing technology is shortening product life, and thus that of the learning curve, while technology, too, is making it possible to produce shorter runs at far lower cost.

Add to these phenomena the segmentation of markets, and the movement upwards in price and quality within these segments, and you have today's and tomorrow's strengthening of the smaller, more specialized producer at the expense of the mass-market mass-producer: the BMW coining D-marks while VW wobbles into losses. But how much smaller is small? In that same car industry, firms can survive on minute output – like Aston Martin, or Lotus, both of which have so far always been able to find new hopefuls to share in their often perilous fortunes.

But the price tag for Aston Martin in January 1981 (£1.25 million on the instalment plan) contrasted tellingly with a price announced the very same month by an equally double-barrelled car company, Daimler-Benz. That very different aristocrat planned to spend a further £30 million, or the price of twenty-four Astons (the company, not the cars), on strengthening its hold on the UK market.

Throughout the decline of its mass car production, Britain has maintained a clutch of minority marques, often (like Astons) of enormous expense, always made in diminutive quantity (Aston once managed eight a week, breathing hard). German manufacturers also know full well how to charge for conspicuous motoring. But their expensive motors are numbered in the thousands, where British makers slay their hundreds.

A national ethos has played a part in the British gravitation towards high-class luxury products with excessively limited markets – a trend clearly visible in the evolution of the Jaguar. Once, it stood on the threshold of Mercedes-Benz scale. It became a strictly exclusive car – with only 6,352 sold on its home market in 1980. This was the inevitable outcome of a journey governed by what can be called the Rolls-Royce Syndrome (with no insult intended): the British preference for making the best, or what the maker fondly believes is the best (not always the same thing), often without regard to economics – while volume sales, and volume profits, are left to lesser breeds.

When a new chief executive, John Egan, saw that there was no future in making Jaguar cars in tiny quantity and infamous quality, dramatic results flowed. Output expanded sharply; quality improved out of all recognition; sales rose strongly all round, above all in the US: and profits leapt ahead, enabling Jaguar to finance things like a £50 million investment programme, centred round robotics, to improve its production still more.

In the desperately over-crowded market in hi-fi, it's too late for the Jaguar technique to work any wonders for the various, mostly tiny British companies which have poured immense ingenuity into developing brilliant products, often very highly priced, for the higher reaches of the market. But their masterpieces were often hard to find in the marketplace, let alone to buy – while the technically inferior (but fast improving) Japanese cleaned up the volume sales.

The Rolls-Royce Syndrome puts product before production: and this policy has been disastrous in market after market. Successful competitors of Britain's have shown that high prices can go hand-in-hand with high output – and even with higher quality. That's because, with modern techniques, efficient production has much more effective quality control built in. And in these days, without quality, the marketing task is increasingly difficult, not to say impossible, for firms of any size, be their economies of scale never so large.

Small Share = Small Profits

But is larger scale, in any case, redundant when it comes to the vital matter of making profits? Reporting in the *Guardian* on a *Harvard Business Review* study, Hamish McRae seized on its suggestion 'that businesses with a small market share can be just as profitable as ones with a large market share'. Hallelujah, indeed: since Britain's market share in all too many world markets is small to infinitesimal, that would have been the best UK business news since Arkwright invented the textile industry. As McRae observed, conventional wisdom – which, in this case, holds that large share equals large profits – often makes better sense stood on its head. But not this time, alas.

For a start, the study, by two Purdue University professors, found only 40 low-share, high-return businesses – out of a total of 649. All 649, moreover, were part of larger parent companies, and thus had a less hostile environment than an own-two-feet firm as they followed essentially conservative policies: standardized products, rare product changes, little sales support, frequently purchased industrial products, and high value-added areas. They didn't (for which you might as well read 'couldn't') compete across the board. Even if they couldn't win on quality (which they tried to do), they generally charged low prices.

On the study's own findings, this is a minority strategy that only works in a minority of cases. As an attack on the Big is Beautiful school, it makes little dent. The BIB theory, as it happens, has far more serious defects. As noted, in an age of fragmentation in technology and markets, having the largest share of, say, European polyethylene sales may be more incubus than asset. Specialization is being forced even on giants because of the inroads made by smaller, concentrated companies with (apparently) small market shares.

But an elementary question in marketing is: How do you define the market? McRae says that Daimler-Benz and BMW were often cited by BL's Sir Michael Edwardes as 'examples of successful medium-sized companies', and Chrysler as a disaster, despite its 'relatively large share of the market'. The latter has never won much more than 15 per cent of US sales: but if you define the great German firms' bailiwick (as you must) as the expensive executive saloon market, they are dominant in Europe and have been for years. Unlike the forty low-share winners in the *HBR* study, these firms are innovative, high-priced, consumer marketers.

There is, however, a catch. What if the specialized, concentrated firm finds itself locked into a segment from which the growth and the glory have fled? A very early exponent of specialization was BSR, which at one point had 50 per cent of the world record-changer market. Unfortunately, this share was all at the low-priced end: BSR depended on economies of scale to give it unbeatable costs, and become the sacrificial victim when recession decimated the low-priced record-player business – and when much of what was left moved decisively up-market.

As it all but collapsed, BSR had the rare experience, in these inflationary times, of a sharp fall in turnover – which in 1981 dropped back all the way to the 1977 level. But then, under the leadership of two entrepreneurs from Hong Kong, BSR changed the whole nature of its business. Its once huge base in turntables had shrunk much too far to support a major company : from 48 per cent of turnover in 1980 to a mere quarter. Hence the big and quite impressive push into growth markets in electronics (almost all of the non-consumer variety and mainly served from the Far East), which made BSR once again a stock market star and virtually created a new company, a Phoenix rising from the ashes of the old.

The Three Clouds Theory

Small, depending on circumstances, can be hideous, even for a firm which has one of the proudest possessions in consumer marketing, a fine old English brand name – like, say, Robertson Foods in jams. The very words Golden Shred, the very image of that golliwog, should practically bring tears to the eyes of pre-war generations. That's the first of the clouds which every silver lining possesses. Nostalgia makes for nice TV commercials, but consumer franchises need continuous up-dating. Otherwise the fine old English firm will inevitably bury its fine old customers.

Cloud Number Two may pile up on the horizon whether the brand is rejuvenated or not. The most paradoxical injustice of all, alas, is that the more successful the brand, the greater its attraction to richer groups wishing to get richer still. After much grunting and groaning, Robertson was expecting to produce pre-tax profits of £2.4 million in the year when its independence was attacked; in 1977–8 it earned £2.7 million, and neither figure exactly excites the tastebuds in relation to the £4.2 million which Avana, shortly before swallowing the unwilling Robertson, earned on *half* the latter's £85 million of sales.

But is the second cloud as threatening as it seems? In the current mood of management, size no longer has any friends. But small may not only lack economic beauty and adequate defence against recessions and predators; it may be hopelessly weak against competitors and supermarket buyers. It's no coincidence that the pitiful array of so-called new products that win space and sales in the supermarkets these days come almost exclusively from big companies. Small business fans have good reason to fear that bad, large company money (and muscle) will drive out small, good firms.

Managements in the lower-size echelons are left with little option. Either you develop the business to the stage where it can be sold to a large group as a thriving, growing concern for much fine gold – and not picked up from the receiver, like the sad canner Lockwood Foods (which failed despite sales of £55 million); or else you build your own well-spread, broadly based group. But that's where the third cloud appears. Companies centred round fine old English brands seldom generate within their management ranks the talent required for creating a genuinely successful multi-product, multi-market, let alone multi-national group. Besides, the effort always entails a question that is hard to answer, especially after long years of success in a single market; what do we do for an encore?

The answer is often made harder still by the problems that tend to creep up on the base business as management makes weak diversifying efforts to dodge these three clouds. In its fateful year, Robertson's profits would have looked far sweeter without the £800,000 rationalization costs incurred (of course) in its basic preserves business: not a very golden piece of Shredding. Yet the Three Clouds Theory isn't immutable. The way out is maximum exploitation of the base market. The more money and skills the company builds in this manner, the higher the probability that the company, having made an optimal success out of one market segment, will have the management capacity (in both senses) to build a similar success in another.

Thus Nippon Kogaku was hit in mid-1983 by an 11 per cent fall in sales of Nikon cameras, partly because of worldwide conditions, partly because it was by then sub-optimizing its innovatory and technology-leading strengths. But in the palmier, optimal days, Nikon had diversified on the back of its optimal skills. Thus, it could partly fall back on a 97 per cent rise in equipment for making semi-conductors and a 32.5 per cent advance in optical measuring instruments. By the same token Asahi Optical, unable to conjure any

growth out of Pentax cameras, recorded a 48 per cent rise in CAD/
CAM (computer-aided design and manufacture) equipment.

Six Points for Small Success

Whichever way you look, the lesson is the same: to win the benefits of
smallness, naked marketers must be as good as, or better than, the
large – and that is by no means so easy as it has sometimes been made
to sound. To return to the *Harvard Business Review* study of successful
low-share companies mentioned earlier, the smaller you are, the more
you may have to avoid what seem like the most desirable markets:
those with high growth, innovation, differentiation, etc. Instead, the
smaller business may be better advised to seek a low profile.

The two Purdue professors who wrote the study (Carolyn Y. Woo
and Arnold C. Cooper) argue that high-growth markets are turbulent
arenas – meaning that all competitors try to grab share leadership, and
competition gets intense. With rapid product and process changes, the
uncertainty gets worse: and the inevitable shake-out follows, with
weak competitors forced to the wall. When the market stops growing
and goes into retreat, the turbulence starts all over again. Mature,
though non-declining, markets with low real growth seem to provide
a more stable environment, in which there is less elbowing to gain
share.

As for frequent product changes, everybody in an industry may
have to spend heavily on launching products as well as on research and
development: and that's difficult for smaller businesses, with less
revenue available. The faster the change, too, the earlier you have to
scrap production tools and dies – and maybe before their useful lives
run out. The professors were surprised to find, too, that 72.5 per cent
of successful low-share performers 'competed in markets
characterized by standard products'. That kind of market, however,
lets you focus your strategies, so that you don't run into the costs of
providing custom-built products or special services.

Then, why do industrial components and supplies dominate –
representing 70–80 per cent of successful low-share performers in the
sample? It's because 'purchase decisions for industrial products are
based largely on performance, service and cost'. So expensive
advertising is usually less important, while, in addition, the purchasers
of industrial products frequently like to operate on contracts. With a

guaranteed market, the seller is better placed to project sales volume, capital spending – and costs. The more often products are bought, too, the less important market share appears to be. Also, the faster a product turns over, the less working capital is likely to be needed.

With a small share, though, a company needs high added value, because that means margins wide enough to absorb cost increases from suppliers or to carry price declines when markets weaken. Also, when value-added is high, there are plenty of opportunities for giving a product different characteristics to mark it out from the herd. It also needs focus – don't try to do everything, but select carefully what you *are* going to do. It must go for quality – special performance and reliability are the only real safeguard. It must compete on price – medium to low relative prices usually go hand-in-hand with the kind of market position described. It must keep costs low – that should be relatively easy when concentrating on a narrow line of standardized products and spending less on product R&D, advertising, promotion, sales force support and new product introduction.

However, it's no easy matter to combine a low market share (meaning less than a fifth of the combined output of the three largest competitors) with high profitability. There's a general rule, so other studies suggest, that 'a difference of ten percentage points in market share is accompanied by a difference of about five points in pre-tax return on investment'. A company can buck the rule; but that will be hard work – and, in some circumstances (say the advent of new, well-financed competition), dangerous work, at that. But look at these necessities again: high added value, differentiation, close focus, quality, competitive pricing, low costs. That is a six-point plan for marketing success on any scale, in any business.

Heller's Golden Rules

HOW TO . . .

. . . STAY VIABLE
1: Never do the uneconomic, even for apparently economic reasons
2: Don't confuse the highest market share with the highest success
3: Don't bet on miracles unless the numbers add up

... BALANCE THE BUSINESS

1: Remember that sales potential isn't determined by capacity, but by the market

2: Avoid being heavily oversold, lest you become heavily overproduced

3: To bring supply and demand into balance, operate first on supply

... MAXIMIZE PROFITS

1: Recognize that price leadership is no good without cost leadership

2: Make production cost and marketing returns two side of the same coin

3: Charge what the traffic will bear – which means finding that out

... ORIENT THE COMPANY

1: Manage for the market, not for the owners

2: Look after the customers, and the finances will start to look after themselves

3: Invest in pursuing only viable shares in viable markets

... GUARANTEE SUCCESS

1: Build quality into manufacture – and into the whole business

2: Never rely on economies of scale as a defence

3: Whether your share is high or low, you need the same six things: high added value, differentiation, close focus, quality, competitive pricing and low costs

SECTION FOUR
IDENTITY

1: Honest to Goodness

In the age of the Naked Market, it's become commonplace that some are more naked than others – the better-clothed others being the great and increasingly dominant retailers. Their huge strength at the sharp end is wielded both through the national brands, which cannot live without the big retailers' national distribution, and through the latter's own-brand strength: the combined weight has radically altered the balance of power in a marketplace which will consequently never be the same again.

But the retailers haven't succeeded by the natural, unassisted working of economic forces. The successful stores have won their increased power deservedly: in the past fifteen years, which have seen a paucity of new British consumer goods firms breaking into the big time, and none too many new big-time consumer brands, the good retailers have produced performances ranging from the solid (Marks & Spencer and GUS) to the undoubtedly spectacular (Sainsbury's and Asda).

There are plenty of other cases to show how the best shopkeepers of Britain have deployed the consistent blend of strategy and tactics, image and range that too many of their suppliers have never got right – and some of their retail competitors, too. Retailing has seen its declines and falls, as well – none more glaring than the fall of F. W. Woolworth. Every now and again some new man at the helm of what, in 1966, was Britain's eighth largest company of any kind would whisper in some sympathetic journalist's ear of the new wonders of Woollies – yet, in 1981, the chain occupied sixty-third place: market value, 40 per cent of Sainsbury's.

Remembering that, in 1966, the latter was only a developing

supermarket chain confined to its south-east patch, and Woolworth's a giant national operation, something very odd must have happened. It's true that the Woolworth's stores, even though many of the innumerable sites were superb High Street pitches, couldn't make a living on the old policy: every low-priced item you might possibly want to buy, from nails to notepaper. But at least the old Woolworth's had a marketing image, although it was increasingly obsolete and uneconomic. In the years thereafter, Woolworth's management never seemed to form a clear, continuous idea of what business it was in: where it did take initiatives, trying superstores or food, it came nowhere near the performance in these same sectors of an Asda or an M&S.

The secrets of failure can be harder to find than those of success. But the top British retailers, the ones which shone in *Management Today*'s comparison of the 100 top companies of 1966 and 1981, are all closely identified with either a family or a small group of commercially motivated managers – like those who launched British Home Stores on the path from eighty-ninth to thirty-ninth position. That has always been one missing ingredient in Woolworth's: the central, individual drive that retailing, an intensely personal business, always requires. Without it the retail life can be terribly hard, even in a nation of shopkeepers and even in a market where the war has been swinging the retail trade's way.

But there's more to it than the family touch – as demonstrated by the fact that it wasn't only Woolworth's that was left mangled in a battle it should have won. Not long after the chain was sold ignominiously to a consortium, Woolworth's was joined in the list of losers by UDS. Its carcase was taken apart in a takeover struggle between a group led by Heron's Gerald Ronson and the eventual victor, Hanson Trust. Slowly, it seemed, the white elephants of British retailing were being picked off (or on) one by one. The process was the inevitable result of the long-standing anomaly just mentioned – the enormous discrepancy between the retail stars and (to switch animal metaphors) the dogs. The contrast is crushing: in the 1982 *Management Today* Growth League, where J. Sainsbury came eighteenth, and even the massive M&S was ninety-eighth, Woolworth's and UDS brought up the rear at (by bizarre coincidence) joint 192nd.

That was the outcome of ten years in which, despite sales higher by

119

166 per cent and 185 per cent respectively, the turgid twain had reduced their long-suffering shareholders' capital by a nominal half – and by far more in real terms. Statistics in these cases don't lie: they merely mirror the well-known fact that, in a High Street world undergoing sensational and rapid evolution, neither group could adjust to the times.

The Importance of Being True

Generalities aside, UDS and Woolworth's appeared to have nothing in common. The latter was the UK subsidiary of the American chain which, in fairly grisly trouble of its own, sealed the British end's fate by selling its stake; the former sprang from the management takeover, by the Lyons tailoring family, of another of those dynastic retailing groups which burgeoned between the wars. The story is uncannily akin to that of the Jacobsons, who obliged similarly at Burton – and then also fell fatefully behind.

The retail discrepancies thus can't just be explained by need of the family touch, à la Sainsbury or Sieff. Obviously some families, like some managers, are more equal than others. But another fundamental truth is that the roots of trouble in the 1980s were put down during the successes of much earlier days. The way in which Woolworth's and the great multiple tailors expanded set patterns of development and trading from which only a marketing magician could ultimately have escaped. The resulting chains by 1980 had too many shops, with too many of them the wrong size and in the wrong places. In contrast with the 1,000 shops of UDS, Marks only had around 250 stores during its fabulous post-war growth, while Sainsbury, at the point when UDS collapsed, had a mere 228.

Put simply, fighting the past as well as the highly competitive present would have defeated abler men than those running Woolworth's and UDS. The winners were, as it happens, far more able. But the people at Sainsbury's, for example, were not called upon for feats of supermarket supermanagement. While good retailing demands much expertise and many essential techniques, the matters are not of baffling complexity. For instance, it is axiomatic that, unless a shopkeeper knows what is selling where (sales analysis), he can't make intelligent decisions or maximize turnover and profits. But Woolworth's conducted no such analysis: in other words, it was as far

120

behind the times.in retailing technique as it was in High Street trading.

But technique alone didn't make the successes. A chain of shops is a brand. Its strength depends on how the brand is perceived – on what makes the shopper enter one store rather than another, and keep on coming back, as the ultimate repeat purchaser. The best store chains have built the best markets, those that last longest and pay most, by being *true*: Trustworthy, Recognized, Unique, Efficient. These champions of the primary marketplace are recognized as different – nobody confuses M&S with Sainsbury's, or either with Tesco: a chain that has had more difficulty, because of its cut-price, small-store origins, in developing the same *true* strength of image.

Note that the image, while personal, is not bound up with personality. Few retailers have dominated an organization as Simon Marks once dominated M&S: but hardly anybody can have thought, even then, that he was buying from Lord Marks, as opposed to Marks & Spencer. No businessman in the kingdom has a better track record than Sir John Sainsbury: but hardly any of his shoppers have the faintest idea who he is. What the great retailers have achieved is what all marketers must strive for: a prominent, pervasive, profitable identity attached, not to the man, but the machine. M&S sells more of some lines than the rest of Britain's retailers put together, solely because all its stores, at all times, are trusted to sell top-quality items at top-value prices that will never, in any particular, depart from what is expected of a product sold by that company.

Retailing's Five Questions

The principles of retail stardom are not confined, though, to chains which number their outlets in the hundreds and their values in the billions. You couldn't better the exposition of the meaning of modern retailing given by Gerry Taylor, a toy retailer who began twenty-five years ago with one shop in Hemel Hempstead, and built up to a total of ten shops, mostly in the counties just north of London, with a 1983 turnover of some £5 million. He concentrates on what he calls the 'cut-and-thrust side' of the business – that is, the High Street shop located as close to the multiples as rents will allow, and aiming for a high turnover with a low profit margin. That is his clear answer to the first crucial question: What kind of business are you running – or do you want to run?

Having made up his mind on that point, as above, Taylor considers what to carry. As he says, 'If you're aiming for a large High Street turnover, you *must* stock certain of the ranges. If you don't, people will be entitled to ask "What kind of a [toy] shop do *they* think they are?!"' Those ranges must form the solid basis of stock (and sales). Which is the answer to question two: What do you *have* to do, like it or not, to retain a strong position in the marketplace?

The matter can't be left at that. There are always alternatives – in Taylor's case, whether to stock the *whole* range or not. He comes down heavily on *not*. He notes that you can obtain as much volume and profit by selecting from a range as by taking the whole of it. 'Some of the major retailers, in fact, run on very limited selections from ranges, trying to avoid padding out with items of slow turnover.' Lying somewhere midway between them and the specialist, Taylor can't afford to do that. So he runs through the whole range and then counts 'the number of lines I've selected. If that turns out more than I wanted, I cut back by eliminating what I believe will be slower-sellers.' That is his answer to question three: Are you applying selectivity to the business – deliberately choosing what you will offer and what you won't?

Almost certainly, the retailer who does not apply selectivity is wasting resources and not getting the optimum bang per buck. Taylor is anxious to deny that he's playing safe. 'Quite the reverse. I believe in taking risks. If you've never lost money on a risk, then you're not buying properly. After all, the riskier items almost always carry a bigger profit margin.' His point is, though, that rewards should be commensurate with risks. The successes will then compensate you for the inevitable failures. Question four is therefore: Are you taking reasoned risks which, if they come off, will make a major contribution?

The third category Taylor goes for is a speciality item – something unique to his business: that meant telescopes in 1983. 'Expensive? Yes. Chance of many sales? No. But a telescope makes a very effective crowd-puller for the window display. The profit margin is good. Manufacturers of such items are happy to replace on a one for one basis. And there's always the chance that any enthusiasts in the area will keep coming back to the shop.' Question five is thus another one which has to be answered: What unique speciality do you have that marks you out from the pack and helps establish your image?

The five questions and their correct answers apply, of course, to any marketing business, not just stores (let alone just toy stores). The good marketer follows the Taylor principles: he knows what he's doing, draws up his own rules from experience, and works hard at getting the results he wants. The great retail chains do no differently. Their national reputation, like Taylor & McKenna's local one, is founded on being *true*; to repeat: Trustworthy, Recognized, Unique, Efficient. That's a truth that the best suppliers to the best retailers, as well, have long known to be as much their own best policy as honesty itself.

2: The Message Is the Medium

The power of advertising as a marketing tool has never been doubted by either its defenders or its critics. The latter believe that ads can actually persuade people, by some form of mass hypnosis, to act against their own interests, to buy what they don't want, watch what they don't wish to see, even vote for candidates they don't really prefer. If only it were that easy. . . .

The marketer, using advertising in the battle for sales, knows that this promotional technique, for all its power, is like patriotism – not enough. That isn't only because alternative means of promotion can be just as effective. Indeed, one of the world's most elegant brand leaders, Moët et Chandon, performs beautifully *sans* advertising, relying solely on heavy spending on other forms of promotion 'below the line'. The problem is rather that even effective advertising can be rendered redundant by badness anywhere: from poor product to dire distribution.

What does 'effective' mean in this context, though? Some of the criteria used to answer that crucial question don't really pass effective muster themselves. Take, for example, the findings produced by advertising agency Allen Brady and Marsh in support of its campaign, 'The Wonder of Woolworth', which first appeared on British TV in 1975. Before ABM took over the advertising, spontaneous recall by viewers asked if they had seen the store chain's advertisements used to run at a microscopic 1 per cent. Only a year after the campaign began, the recall sprang to 75 per cent. Six years on, apparently, the figure had reached still more Himalayan heights – 86 per cent, no less.

Did this spectacular increase in impact improve Woolworth's business to match? From 1975 to 1982 sales indeed grew by 128 per

124

cent to £1.05 billion (against, however, 228 per cent for Marks & Spencer). But margins, 10.4 per cent in 1973–4, were only 7.1 per cent in the first Wonder Year. They bumbled along in the sevens until 1980–1, and then nose-dived: 5.4 per cent, 3.6 per cent – and a loss in the first quarter of 1982. Either the campaign manfully prevented the fall from being still more fearful; or it wasn't effective advertising, in the sense that it didn't successfully encourage consumers to buy the right, higher-margin goods from the stores; or the fault lay with the way Woolworth's itself was managed.

None of the three alternatives is mutually exclusive. The clue may lie in the agency's view, expressed in a panegyric to its own wonders, that 'The real truth about Woolworth, the truth to be *advertised*, was that Woolworth was a wonderland of variety, an Aladdin's Cave, a cornucopia.' Well, it wasn't: the product belied the promise. Woolworth's High Street stores resembled Aladdin's Cave about as closely as the Politburo does Snow White and the Seven Dwarfs. Woolworth was stuck with self-evident problems of merchandise, display and service of the kind that can't be washed away by all the advertising that money can buy. Those basic issues, not those of advertising, are where M&S clobbered Woolworth's all over the shops.

The aftermath of the profit collapse, as noted in the previous chapter, was that the chain's American parents sold their stake, and a new consortium took over the reins; then, among other changes, ABM lost the account, Wonder of Woolworth and all. Unfair though this must have seemed to the agency, it was an understandable reaction to the lack of success in the marketplace. Even highly 'effective' advertising, judged by the criterion of recall, cannot, whatever advertising's critics may think, take the customer to water – let alone make him or her drink.

The Magnificent Seven

The agency in this context was researching into the wrong subject, although it was certainly right to be doing research. Many marketers don't. Indeed, why marketing companies so often misuse or mistrust research is one of those mysteries, like vanishing ships in the Bermuda Triangle, that are impossible to solve. One common excuse – implicit or explicit – is precisely that research can't measure the imponderables,

125

especially in 'creative' areas like advertising. The view is poppycock: and there's the word of a creative genius to prove it. Writing in the *Harvard Business Review* with an agency colleague, Joel Raphaelson, the great David Ogilvy, founder of Ogilvy and Mather, discusses research to profound effect.

Only by research can you find out, for example, whether it's a good business idea to build an advertising campaign around a celebrity. It sounds like an excellent notion, and there's a long history of such campaigns, ranging from soap endorsements by pre-war society beauties to Sir Freddie Laker's Skytrain ads. But the research shows that, although the celebrity ads scored 22 per cent *above* average recall, they changed consumer brand preference 21 per cent *less* than the average of advertisements studied.

The reason for the discrepancy is less important than the conclusion. (In fact, what happens is that attention gets focused on the celebrity, not the product.) The attitude of the consuming public to the advertising isn't the point. That lies only in the reaction displayed at the point of sale. The shift in brand preference is the truly vital measure, and even more significant than may appear at first sight.

According to Raphaelson and Ogilvy, the research found that viewers who changed brands bought the product concerned 3.3 times more often than non-changers. O. and R. of O. and M. cite these Magnificent Seven shifters:

1. Problem solution.

2. Humour ('when the humour is pertinent to the selling proposition'). ·

3. Relevant characters ('personalities, developed by the advertising, who become associated with a brand').

4. Slice-of-life ('enactments in which a doubter is converted').

5. News ('new products, new ideas, new information').

6. Candid camera testimonials.

7. Demonstrations.

Thus the reason why Gloria Vanderbilt, the heiress and society figure, proved so brilliant a choice to promote (and name) designer jeans is that she was a 'relevant character' – who became much more famous by being associated with the advertising and the brand. The brilliance, moreover, lay partly in the fact that 'Vanderbilt' is something of a brand in itself, immediately suggestive of the smartness and wealth which the lady embodied.

The Magnificent Seven are a concise and clear guide to preference-shifting ads – and what O. and R. have to say is none the worse for its lack of earth-shattering information. In fact, the rules of successful advertising, like those for all successful business, are simplicity itself. If you want your ads to work, use cartoons and animation to reach children – not grown-ups. Avoid many short scenes and changes of situation. Words on the screen ('supers') are super, but only if they reinforce the main point. Show the package – and always end with the brand name. Start with the key idea – and so on.

The same obviousness applies to the rules on cold print: for instance, as in TV, press ads with 'news' score above average; it pays to show the product in use and the end result of having used it; 'copywriters who believe they can tease readers into reading an advertisement are throwing money away' – and so on. Yet you only need to glance at a TV or colour magazine to see flagrant breaches of the obvious rules.

The truth is that too many managers think themselves wiser than any research finding and more knowledgeable, when it comes to promoting their product, than any advertising agent. They thus encourage the very split, between 'pure' advertising and the impure world of the naked market, which produces schizophrenia about what is and isn't effective. The truth to remember at all times is that advertising which isn't *commercially* effective is a waste of money; and that effectiveness can be and certainly must be measured where it counts – in the marketplace.

Practise What You Promise

The research may, of course, demonstrate that no advertising can be particularly effective in a particular market. Banking could be an example. Choice of bank may be influenced predominantly by quite extraneous factors – like where Father banked, or even location: which brings to mind a BP study, made long ago, that demonstrated fairly conclusively that, in anything but the short term, for all the intensive hullaballoo of the petrol marketers, the dominant force determining share of market was simply the siting of service stations. The same phenomenon almost certainly takes place in banking. All those jolly advertising campaigns probably cancel each other out to a considerable extent. While it then becomes imperative for each bank

127

to maintain its 'share of voice', the total vocalization doesn't add a penny to the total of deposits or profits.

Any research which confirmed the above probabilities would therefore doubtless share the fate of the BP study mentioned above. Nobody would take the blindest bit of notice, especially if the whole industry is engaged in a bout of highly visible competition. The banks have been conspicuous among institutions once innocent of marketing in their subsequent wholesale conversion (at least in principle) to the religion. Whether the new disciplines or diversions have made much difference to the competitive battle is hard to determine. Among the prime objects of marketers are to win more (profitable) customers, and to win more (profitable) business from the latter, partly by introducing more (profitable) products. To the extent that the latter – new banking products – have swayed the struggle, advertising has certainly been indispensable. No better method exists of blazoning forth and explaining the virtues of an innovation – and there have, of course, been highly significant innovations in this market.

The most notable is certainly the bank credit card, pioneered by the always formidable Bank of America in California, and picked up in Britain by the relatively agile Barclays. Since both are the biggest in their own markets, this proves that, at least in the world of financial marketing, the race doesn't have to go to the small and swift. But financial products have one great defect: they are far too easily imitated. In the very nature of banking, one man's innovation rapidly becomes another man's imitation. When every competitor can afford to match the competition on every point, none can hope to gain a lasting advantage from a new product, any more than from a new advertising campaign.

In circumstances like these, the use of advertising is fundamentally strategic. The spender should lay out the least money necessary to reinforce positive emotions among existing and potential customers – feelings which can also be measured by intelligent research. The research can also show how the bank, or any other organization, ranks against its competitors. But at the end of the day, as with Woolworth's, it's the reality that counts. The banks' most powerful marketing weapon is probably the oldest one of all – standards of customer service. And since truth and honesty are essential ingredients of the above, it doesn't help for an institution (in this case, the Midland)to advertise itself as 'the friendly bank' – and then for one of its branches to have an overdrawn student arrested. The Wonder of Woolworth syndrome works in all situations: advertising invariably contains and conveys a promise, and the promise must be kept.

The Magnificent Seven techniques recommended by Ogilvy and Raphaelson, if closely examined, clearly support the giving of authentic promises in an authentic manner. The good marketer offers a real solution to a genuine problem, and does so with pertinent humour, using only relevant characters in authentic 'slice-of-life' situations, stressing news of new properties, using believable testimonials, and demonstrating how the product works. True, these strategies lead to the endless series of housewives being shown how to remove dirty marks from clothes and sinks – the very mind-numbing commercials to which advertising's critics object.

But the marketers who run soap companies don't run these ads because they are unable to think of anything else. It is because of the proven effectiveness of this particular sales approach. But the effectiveness though, as with bank or petrol advertising, must be diluted if all soap companies are on the same tack. That offers a glittering prize to the innovative marketer who can break the industry mould. He's most unlikely to break it, however, by breaking the rules of truly effective advertising – and he'll never do it unless his claim and the actuality actually match.

3: The Offer They Can't Refuse – You Hope

At least one thing is sure about advertising: it is supposed to be true, honest, and fair – and if it isn't, due opprobrium will be heaped on the perpetrator's head. But what about the rest of marketing? In a perfect world – or market – only the true, fair, and just would prevail. But in the real, imperfect world, marketing is rife with tricks, dirty and otherwise, by which companies seek to achieve a decidedly unfair advantage over others.

Nor are governments in much of a position to cluck tongues and hand out demerits – for they are sometimes the dirtiest tricksters of all, none more so than the French. Even by Gallic standards, the Poitiers Ploy of 1983 was a remarkable piece of untrue, unfair, and unjust interference with the free market: in this case, that for video cassette recorders. Confronted with an unwelcome influx of VCRs, the French authorities decided that, from then on, all import controls on the offending objects would be carried out by the customs post at the commercially obscure town of Poitiers.

In no way, *bien sur*, did this contravene the rules of GATT (the General Agreement on Trade and Tariffs), the principles of fair play or the ideals of free trade. It was true, of course, that with four officials and no computer, Poitiers would take forever to clear VCR shipments. Otherwise Sony, JVC *et al* were left at perfect liberty to flood the French market with their products – machines, incidentally, which the French didn't make at all.

It would be a mistake, though, to assume that marketers in other lands were steaming with righteous indignation over the Poitiers principle, as opposed to its practice. That includes the sinned-against Japanese; when it comes to excluding unwanted machines (or anything else), they are dyed in the deepest villainy. As for British marketers, they are more likely to complain, not about the perfidious French, but about the barmy British, who don't do likewise. Fools that they are, Brits play by the rules, while the French (and the Japanese) make up the rules as they go along. Thus when the French once decreed that any quality labels had to receive prior government approval, it turned out that the Gallic definition of quality included (*naturellement*) 'Made in France'.

Before concluding that Whitehall should undergo a crash course in cheating, it's sensible to ask what benefits arise from protectionism, covert or overt. The answer depends on whether or not the protected industry is internationally competitive, or is moving in that direction. If not (on either or both counts), a protectionist policy gets you nowhere: it merely forces the local consumer to pay more for worse goods. If the industry is competitive, or is making genuine progress in that direction, protecting it is superfluous in the first case and dangerous in the second — dangerous because the protection will reduce the competitive stimulus. France is an excellent proof of the argument. For all its protectionism, in which world car markets are French imports the leaders? And how was it that the French electronics industry was so battered and backward that it wasn't making VCRs at all?

Those who retort by pointing to the Japanese juggernaut are misled. There's no evidence that the Japanese would have fared any less well in cameras, motorcycles, hi-fi, cars, TV, etc. if they hadn't played the Poitiers Ploy on so grand — and silly — a scale. As economist Henry George wrote, 'What protectionism teaches us is to do to ourselves in time of peace what enemies do to us in time of war.' All the same, it requires virtue and fortitude beyond the nature of man to suffer the protectionist blows of others without striking back. Few firms, anyway, can resist the temptation of getting from government what they can't get from the marketplace.

In Government's Gift

For example, in the same business of VCRs, the Philips-Grundig combination tried the Brussels Bash instead of the Poitiers Ploy — hoping that a Common Market anti-dumping investigation would ease its pains. The background to this agony was that Grundig had been forced to cut the price of its most expensive VCR by a third, only to find outdated Japanese machines undercutting even its reduced price by nearly half. The German distress – Grundig had high hopes of badly needed salvation invested in its VCRs – is fully understandable. But that's not the real point. The truth revolves around two questions. One, are Sony, Matsushita, and JVC really selling below factory cost? Two, is their domination of the Euromarket, however achieved, good or bad?

On the first point, more than one highly competitive consumer durable firm has been shocked to find Japanese rivals undercutting its pride and joy. Dumping, naturally, is the first thought in these circumstances. But when detailed investigation is set in train it often reveals that the Japanese are charging a full and fair ex-factory price. In VCRs, where they have 90 per cent of the world market, it would be amazing if Japanese manufacturers didn't command much higher efficiencies than Grundig-Philips.

But that's not all. That 90 per cent share also reflects a shamingly more successful marketing effort. The West European partners, for all their native strengths, were left at the post by competitors based thousands of miles away from markets which Grundig and Philips should have sewn up with steel thread. After so monumental a failure, the twain's dumping accusations inevitably looked like the last refuge of the unsuccessful: a bad move for the consumer, and one of doubtful benefit to themselves.

Instead of trying to defend an indefensible position in this current boom sector, the two would have been far better advised to concentrate their efforts on the next hot consumer product. But who would you expect to father that coming innovation? The same people, no doubt, who first brought the European consumer the portable hi-fi, the VCR, the micro hi-fi, the lightweight headphone, etc., etc. – and their names were not Philips or Grundig. Against sheer failure to innovate effectively, protectionism is no protection.

The unfair advantages in government's gift, however, go far beyond protectionism – which explains why the business of lobbying politicians and civil servants has become so big and lucrative, especially in the US. But even in Britain, a giant like ICI has shown itself to be no mean hand down the years in the political lobbies, whose goings-on seldom surface – though when they do, as in the summer of 1982, the insight is revealing.

In effect, ICI revealed that it had been out-lobbied by Shell, Esso, and BP. The latter three had won large tax concessions (granted, it was said, to save new plants in the always politically sensitive area of Scotland) enabling them to undercut ICI's raw material cost by more than half. In ghastly market conditions like those for most petrochemicals at the time, with prices ground down by over-capacity, no marketing strategem visible to the naked eye could offer any comparable prospect of winning competitive advantage. All that ICI could do in these conditions, private pressure having failed, was to go public and assail the government, threatening to shut its Teesside complex, 9,000 jobs and all, if it didn't get fair play. But this is the sort of boot that can easily change feet: how much advantage has ICI gathered down the years from more successful close encounters of the usual kind with government?

Preferential purchasing, of course, is a form of internal protectionism, and one which, in the case of computers, has driven IBM to much distress – with public contracts reserved in favour of ICL, until the Common Market came to the former's aid. If official Buy British policies aren't available, unofficial ones can always be attempted; this frequently happens with British cars, meaning BL cars – as witness a letter sent to BL suppliers in 1982: 'If someone with whom we do business has a policy of not buying our cars, we would have to review our purchasing policy in relation to that company. . . . In the past, it could have been claimed that our car range left something to be desired. That is no longer the case.' The breathtaking bit of that passage is the threat, about as veiled as a Soho stripper, that UK suppliers who didn't scratch BL's back by buying its cars might well be scratched themselves – if, presumably, BL could find another supplier of equal quality and reliability at the same or a better price. If it couldn't, the company would have been indulging in the old, foolish game of cutting off its nose to spite its face.

Marketing by Muscle in these and even more overt ways is all too common – and, incidentally, the above technique is formally barred by IBM, which won't allow any hint of so-called 'reciprocity' in its buying and selling. Lord Acton's maxim that all power corrupts, and that absolute power corrupts absolutely, applies in marketing, too. That's why the very principle of monopoly is nowadays regarded as against the public interest. Where a powerful company has a lever to pull, it will tend not to resist the temptation to exercise its muscles.

Dishonesty Always Costs

Consider the case of Tudor, a junior rival to the mighty Kodak. A dispute over price ended many years of Tudor buying its well-established own-brand film from 3M – a company which provides Kodak with a big market through High Street processing shoplets. Tudor then switched to another manufacturer. Kodak duly circulated dealers with the news that, because Tudorcolor II films had 'different printing characteristics', it wouldn't handle them on the commercially crucial urgent processing service. As Kodak later admitted, the characteristics were exactly the same as those of films it did so handle.

Whether Kodak's gambit was fair or unfair has now passed into history with the giant's withdrawal from a developing and printing market that 'could no longer be served profitably' at Kodak's level of costs. None of its marketing efforts, fair or unfair, has been able to save Kodak's profits from the impact of lower-cost competition (led by Japan's Fuji) which, as noted, has loosened the American company's hold on world markets.

In the end, all the tricks a company plays by itself (like, ultimately, tricks played by government) will fail in face of the more fundamental forces of markets – although that won't stop either countries or companies from making the effort. In 1983 one of the most remarkable endeavours of this kind was staged by Ford. As the sales battle raged between the Cavaliers of Vauxhall and the rounded Sierras of Ford, the latter resorted, on a larger scale than anybody could recall, to the 'hype', with huge financial inducements offered to force sales through the trade.

The effect of this, and no doubt the object of the exercise, was to boost Ford's apparent market share and thus keep it at the top of the tree. But no degree of hype could offset the fact that the Sierra's sales performance had not matched that of its Cortina predecessor. Even if the odious comparison really reflects the decline of the entire segment, the underlying market situation was worse than Ford has known for years. It had been the unquestioned master of the UK market: first to produce an integrated model range, first to find the right mid-range formula, first to produce and succeed with a pan-European model policy. Its marketing had been equally sure-footed, with carefully researched product design supported by strong promotion, which both reinforced and was reinforced by a Ford brand that had been pushed steadily up the quality ladder as the cars had been upgraded.

What Ford couldn't control, though, was the inaction or reaction of General Motors. That fight against the Cavalier is tougher than any that Ford has fought before, because it stems from the worldwide counter-attack of the vastly richer GM, whose integrated range is designed to make Ford the European underdog. The hyping up of Ford's sales figures reflected, no doubt, what is seen as the vital importance of maintaining the company as Number One against a rapidly growing rival: one which can afford to match Ford almost pound for pound in advertising, despite its smaller share of the market.

The suspicion is that Ford's whole tactical plan in the Sierra's first year was directed internally as well as externally — including an advertising slogan, 'Man and machine in perfect harmony', that, while lacking in meaning to anybody else, may have helped to convince the management that its controversial Sierra concept was correct. Maybe that's part of the function of much marketing by Muscle and Machination: to hide from the management concerned the reality that its hold over the true marketplace has weakened.

The Japanese, being nothing but realistic, will go to any lengths, not to hide their weaknesses, but to repair them. Hence the California Caper, the attempt to steal IBM secrets which raised the possibility that some of Japan's brilliance in world markets rests not on quality circles, or better strategies, or the spirit of Zen — but on simple theft of Western technology. Even more than the other cases recounted, the behaviour of Hitachi in this respect offends against the principles of truth, justice, and fairness. In naked markets these principles usually will be honoured as much in the breach as the observance. But note that dishonesty and dirty tricks always carry a cost — even if it's less than the $300 million which Hitachi allegedly had to pay to IBM. Serve it right.

4: They Hardly Ever Come Back

What's in a name? This is one of the basic questions in marketing, yet one that has seldom had an even partially convincing answer. Brands have names: companies have names. In either case, the names can become almost priceless with time, success and usage. They can, paradoxically, become so well established that they lose all value – becoming generic, like Hoover, describing not so much the particular product, but what it does.

Given that names acquire their worth only with time, though, it's a brave company that throws it away, unless there is a compelling reason for so doing. The compelling reason for staying put, if you can, may be seen from the following question: What do Bestobell, Huntley & Palmers, Berec and Cookson have in common? For most people, the most difficult part of that question can be summed up in two words: Cookson who? It's the new name picked on by Lead Industries, which wanted to escape from its leaden image and (for no apparent good reason) chose to fly instead an old-established subsidiary's colours.

The obvious problem is that it takes time and trouble to build up any recognition in the marketplace for the new name. It helps if, like Associated Biscuits, the company can fasten on its best-known brand, Huntley & Palmers. The difficulty is academic if, as with Bell's Asbestos, the name (because of the asbestos fears and lawsuits) has become unbearable, or at least impossible to bear – hence Bestobell. But the motivation is the crux of the matter.

Take the newly fledged Cookson. In fact, its image was leaden in more ways than one. Over the past decade this company's pre-tax profits had risen by only 133 per cent (a third as fast as sales) and its share price by a mere 34 per cent: not the kind of thing that corporate dreams are made of. Frequently, when managements do start dreaming of higher things, changing the company name seems the easiest place to start.

It is, however, only a start. At its best, the name change can be a signal, within and without the company, of other and more fundamental changes. If the stock market receives the signal loud and clear, then a better reputation can be hung on the new peg, and the company's rating on the exchanges may rise – meaning that its cost of capital (including the cost of acquisitions) will fall.

As a final hope, the company can hope to forge its name into a most powerful marketing tool – merely think of Ford, Heinz, Cadbury, Sony, etc. Making a silk purse like that out of a leaden name isn't possible, although Cookson doesn't sound too promising, either. In any event, that kind of concentrated strength isn't available to a conglomerate. This explains why so many conspicuous cases of the breed have signalled their reform and renaissance by retreating behind letters whose origins most people have now long forgotten – like BOC or BTR. Since such groups are generally known by their initials, anyhow, the transformation is minimal. So long as the transformation of the company is maximal, the change hardly matters.

With the same proviso, it should hardly matter when, à la Huntley & Palmers, a familiar brand takes over from a not very familiar, anonymous corporate name like Associated Biscuits. The marketing logic is clear from what has just been said. Where the company and the brand are one, they can reinforce each other. Which makes it all the more difficult to understand why another problem company, Ever Ready, moved in the opposite direction – abandoning a great brand name in favour of an ugly invention, Berec.

The hideous neologism didn't last long. Transformed only in name, Berec was taken over by Hanson Trust and promptly renamed (or named back) British Ever Ready. It's tempting in hindsight, after this traumatic takeover, to read the old nomenclature as a signal of marketing sin, of a turning away from the product towards less crucial objectives – in this case the worldwide markets, where Berec, translatable or untranslatable into any language, was thought to have a better chance.

The company didn't, though. The product line on which penetration of any market depended had been sorely neglected. Lack of development spending was one of the several reasons why Berec was so vulnerable to the Hanson bid. But it's a curious fact that Berec wasn't the only one of the four funny name changes to receive an unwelcome takeover bid. The same fate befell both Huntley & Palmers and Bestobell (which all but succumbed to BTR). This more than coincidence suggests that the wish to expunge the old corporation from the map betrays some inner lack of confidence, some uncertainty of direction, some experience of past failure.

As it happens, that experience was also true of the renamed companies mentioned above – BOC and BTR – both of which have subsequently been large successes, the latter to an especially spectacular degree. The perceived necessity to change the name reflected past corporate disappointment, particularly severe in the case of BTR, which was in a parlously weak state when transformation began. But if it is a general rule that name changes always spring from weakness, their success or failure plainly depends on how strongly the management exploits the potential of a fresh start.

AE's Lucky Break

The more you think about the proposition that name changes spring from weakness, the more true it seems. For instance, the US firm AM International was Addressograph-Multigraph before the series of calamitous errors which reduced it to so parlous a state that, in a dying spasm, it put on the block seven companies that mainly had only just been bought. The new approach at AM looked sound, though – trying to struggle back to life with just three distinct core activities. Separate and strengthen, divide and conquer; whatever the description, the principle is hard to gainsay. What man has wrongly brought together must be put asunder to make sense.

The weakness which AM concealed beneath its name change is one that besets many putting-together conglomerates. Because the company itself isn't cohesive – say, a batch of businesses clustered loosely round a meat-packing firm called Swift – it is renamed Esmark in the forlorn hope that the new name will make the corporate image more cohesive, if nothing else. When it doesn't, as happened with Esmark, takeover and total disappearance into another company (in this case, another conglomerate, Beatrice Foods) often result.

The same name-to-grave fate seemed inevitably to be coming the way of AE – formerly known as Associated Engineering – when its directors meekly accepted a piddling bid from its biggest UK competitor, the GKN giant. Battered and bloodied by the recession, the AE board had fallen hook, line and sinker for the powerful conventional wisdom – that all markets have become global, that such global markets demand global companies, and that to become global in turn demands global scale.

For that reason, the GKN board was prepared to pay a heavy price (dropping at least a tenth of the combined business as UK customers sensibly went for second sources abroad) to swallow up AE's two initials. All that saved the smaller company from takeover, and gave its awakened directors time to march off smartly in the opposite direction of thought, was the uncovenanted action taken by the Monopolies Commission in considering and then rejecting the whole deal – a lucky break in which AE happily recovered the very identity that it was on the brink of losing for ever.

The company ended up by spunkily challenging the entire GKN view that 'the market for engine parts is already a European market and all national markets are, or are becoming, sub-markets'. In reality, if paradoxically, both sides of the argument were right. It's true that no British manufacturer can hope to survive and thrive (not just in so hotly competitive a field as car components, but also in most other fields) from a national market that has contracted relatively and in some cases absolutely – but that isn't the end of the story.

In the overlap products, AE outweighed the giant by rising three to one. The company's investment in modern technology, AE belatedly realized, had given it the new economies of scale, which potentially are as global as anybody's. True, in today's highly competitive conditions, even the utmost vigilance, concentrating on getting the lowest cost structure, the highest quality image, etc., etc., may not avert the evil decree. But with integration, modernization, spread and diversification, companies by any other name can smell very sweet. Their names only become winners, though, because they are attached to winning companies: the self-same truth that has long been known about winning brands.

The Low Sierra

Sometimes even a winning brand name may have to be sacrificed;

although the go – no–go decision must be one of the most painful in world business. Take Ford's decision to drop the brand–name Cortina when it was still riding high at the top of the mid-priced sector. In the two decades since the Cortina I made its mark, none of its European rivals had been able to mount a convincing challenge. The bestsellers from VW, Renault, Fiat, and GM's Vauxhall-Opel used to be lower down the range, concentrating around or below the zone where Ford locates the Escort. But all that changed after the other majors, especially GM (Cavalier and Ascona), had piled in.

The crucial marketing fact is that Ford saw them coming and concluded that the years of juggling with the Cortina had run their course. While the last of the Cortinas resembled the Mark I about as closely as the Orient Express does a 125 train, the Cortina saga was a masterly demonstration of a rare marketing skill: keeping a broad identity and concept intact while radically changing the product as it leads and responds to the market. The Escort is still on a similar track. But there must be a cumulative loss of freshness, which paradoxically gives the marketer a new weapon – the ability to get freshness on his side with a totally new launch.

While it was a gamble (and, at £660 million, a heavy one) to launch a literally brand-new brand in the Sierra, there was also risk in running yet another series of the Cortina. The new launch, moreover, gave Ford the chance to crack the box-like mould of the mid-priced market and to make further progress in its long uphill pilgrimage up-market, heading for top image and top price.

Critics contended from the start that Ford had gone over the top, outdistancing the market in design and making costly errors in detailing. Be that as it may – and the Sierra's comprehensive outstripping by Vauxhall's Cavalier shows that it may well be – one conclusion was immediately obvious. As I wrote at the time, 'The market pressures are intensifying fast: even though the saga of the Sierra is only just beginning, the days of the High Sierra may be doomed.'

The previous chapter described some of the consequences of that truth. Nobody will ever know how many sales Ford lost by abandoning the Cortina name while it was still at its peak. But peaks do pass – and the common thread binding brand and company names is that they demand constant renewal and reinforcement: that is, the product and its promise must match the package and the projection.

Look after the market, in other words, and the name will look after itself. The fact that Hoover became generic didn't matter so long as the company dominated a growing market in vacuum cleaners. What sabotaged the company was only its own inability to maintain sufficient strength in the appliance market. If success makes names, though, it must follow that names don't make success. That's why corporate name changelings rarely make it back to lost glory. The original failure and the subsequent disappointment reflect a single cause: that loss of natural identity which, in naked markets, so often proves fatal.

5: Lies, Damned Lies – and Self-Deception

Marketing men indulge in exaggeration (or lies) more cheerfully, it seems, than anybody else in management. Often there's no apparent point in these fibs about their market shares, their product's charms, their profits: but nobody apparently minds. The issue is not the same as truth in advertising, something on which everybody is insistent, but which – in all truth – is among the more boring of management issues (witness the worthies who were outraged at the suggestion that Heineken lager really did reach parts that other beers didn't). Truth in marketing actually matters far more, because the foundation of a product's success is its credibility. Whether it is possible to tell the truth, the whole truth, and nothing but the truth is beside the point. Unless the public believes the message conveyed by the product and its promotion, the marketing game is lost.

In some conspicuous cases, though, the promotion stars less the product than the producer, a strategy never illustrated more mordantly than when Sir Freddie Laker spent some of his last hours in command of his doomed airline starring in a TV commercial. Laker had been Britain's most visible exponent of this form of star marketing, in which the businessman himself both provides and promotes the product. Another practitioner of this art form was John Z. De Lorean – and yet another was the washing machine manufacturer, John Bloom.

What did the trio have in common, apart from a penchant for getting into the euphemistic hole known as 'financial difficulties'? They also enjoyed a large size in egos – which makes it difficult to decide whether the marketing method was truly chosen for its supposed efficacy alone. Even if it wasn't, even if the man really revels

142

over seeing his name in lights, the technique could be none the less effective for that. But it has obvious limitations: the rich man's image is purely promotional; it can't of itself contribute much to the image of the mass-market product; it can't contribute anything if the product won't wash.

This criticism doesn't apply to Victor Kiam (see Section Three), whose selling pitch in the Remington ads was not his far from famous self, but a great line – the razor was so good that he bought the whole darned company. What undermined Laker in the marketplace was a credibility weakened by the confusion of its (or his) image as other airlines muscled in on the cheap fares act. 'Standby', not 'Laker', became the synonym for flying cheap – and it's a sign of Laker's own confusion that its final forlorn marketing ploy was a first-class service lumbered with the name of Regency.

Maybe analysis would show that people never fully believe a man's pitch for his own product. But there's little doubt that the pitchman does: the same ego that contributes to those personal displays can blind its owner to the unpleasant realities of his business. Thus the former Rolls-Razor washing machine tsar once announced to the world that 'I've got this John Bloom thing': meaning that the charisma of his personality (about as appetizing as a bar of soap, but never mind) could sell anything to which the Great Name was lent. Shortly after that, Bloom's decline reached the point where the Name couldn't even sell washing machines: and that was that.

Management by Semantics

The pressure to bend the truth, or at least the language, is never greater than when the chips are really down.

Enter Sir Freddie Laker again. Faced with the hard fact that paying back his £130 million debt on schedule would involve an insurmountable degree of financial inconvenience, Laker boldly announced a banking 'innovation': what he called a 'release-and-recapture' clause. In other words, if the banks 'released' him from his obligation to repay them on the due date, they could, lucky things, 'recapture' the money at some later point.

Those who find some difficulty in telling the difference between that and asking for a plain and simple extension of a repayment period don't understand the extreme – and basic – importance of semantics in

143

marketing. Every marketer knows that 'new' is only surpassed in marketing power by 'free': even though most products labelled 'new' are not, and even though everything placarded as 'free' isn't. To elaborate on the latter point, Milton Friedman's book title, *There's No Such Thing as a Free Lunch*, has it right: the New York saloons that once upon a time gave away 'free' meals obviously had to recoup the cost in the price of the booze, or go bust.

That is an ineluctable fact of life and economics. The ineluctability of Laker Airways was that of a classic price-cutting case. Initially, the price-cutter operates and flourishes under the umbrella of the excessive prices charged by the established giants whose prices he is undermining. When, eventually and inevitably, they retaliate, he loses his Unique Selling Proposition and with it some of the sold-out volume which keeps down his unit costs. If (like Laker) he is then left having to finance a mountain of debts (£130 million against group funds of only £23 million), he's in no good position to ride over shocks like 1981's dramatic fall in the pound.

What Laker was trying to do was place the bankers in an exquisite bind. Heads the banks wouldn't win, because disobliging Laker would do their own balance sheets no good: tails, they lost, because acceding to Laker's 'release-and-recapture' fandango would make them seem like reluctant fuddy-duddies dancing to his tune. It can't have been any consolation that the laws of market economics will win in the end, whatever the semantics. Laker and his planes duly went down, rubbing in the point that management by semantics doesn't work: the words must marry the music just as much as (see 3 in this section) the package must match the product.

The Truth Should Out

In a very real sense, the image of the company is a demonstration of the same words-and-music point. The essential, though, is to have an honest company song, and to ensure that it is being heard. Curiously, this self-evident truth isn't heeded by many companies: an oversight dramatically revealed if some predator produces an unwelcome assault – as when BTR attacked Thomas Tilling, which, with no less than twice BTR's sales, should have been invulnerable.

The attack prompted, from the normally unseen and not heard Tilling, a stream of prose poems, expensively published as ads,

144

singing its own praises. The underlying question is fundamentally important. Should companies make a continuous, sustained effort to market themselves? Waiting for a takeover bid to step up self-promotion can't be right. It's a bit late for the fox to take out life insurance when the lead hound has him by the tail. So the answer to the question looks cut and dried. Self-marketing is an essential corporate task, to be conducted with the same due care and attention as the main marketing activity.

That being so (and it's hard to argue otherwise), why is that truth, as noted, so widely ignored? Take BTR itself: few people outside the company, even in so-called informed circles, could tell you much about the group's products or how and where it has created so phenomenal a record of profit-hungry growth. Many gee-whiz companies are content to let the lovely record speak for itself and the media knock at their doors – so the management sees little need to spend real money on marketing the company.

But Catch-22 applies. Suppose the company is *unsuccessful*: it also prefers to keep a low profile – in the fond, foolish hope that the media (and eventually the bad results) will go away. At that latter point, it customarily tries to attract attention to a tale of wondrous recovery; and any journalist knows the ominous implications when a company touting such a tale suddenly goes silent. None of this makes any more sense than refusing to advertise a product because it's selling like hot pop: and then, again, refusing to advertise because sales have slumped too far to justify the expense.

Bid situations often show up the folly. For example, what made Sotheby's, before its white knight came riding to the rescue from Texas, so pathetically vulnerable to the unlikely combination of three Americans called Felt, Swid and Cogan? The auction house had so neglected its self-marketing as to lose many of the large shareholders who should have formed its natural defences. If the product doesn't live up to the claims, that is another argument against silence. Finding out how others see you, and then seeking to correct and improve the perceptions, will inevitably draw attention to the corporate sins and omissions – and increase the chances of rectifying them.

There's one large public company, for example, which only added a finance director to its minuscule board when a public relations firm suggested that the absence thereof would be taken amiss in the City. That appointment, however, hasn't lifted either the company's profile or its performance: self-marketing means far more in terms of PR, strategic policies, image research, corporate identity and marketing, and so on. For lack of these necessities, there are important companies which are little known to consumers, investors, politicians, journalists, even to their own workforce. They can hardly blame fate when it knocks on their door.

Fate can come unbidden, of course. Sometimes, market misfortune doesn't rain – it pours. No sooner had Dista Products emerged from the major mishap (and mishandling) of the forced withdrawal of Opren, its anti-arthritic offering, than it was plunged into renewed controversy over its pain-killing Distalgesic. This rumpus is an even graver matter for Dista (which belongs to the US giant Eli Lilly) than the Opren calamity. The latter is (or was) comparatively new, but the analgesic had contributed heavily to Dista for years: at £10 million of UK sales and 15 per cent of the market, it was no mean money spinner.

Distalgesic was in double trouble, under attack for being allegedly dangerous and, anyway, no more effective than good old non-prescription paracetamol. But Dista's reactions didn't demonstrate full awareness that, if a product is accused of being killing (as opposed to just pain-killing), the makers must not only ensure that it isn't – they must be seen to be doing so. Any hint of stonewalling or concealing unsatisfactory evidence may cook your market goose. Thus the asbestos industry, by reacting too slowly to fears about the product, helped to create a situation of total distrust, in which lunatic precautions were being taken over risks that may be less than those of sitting in a smoke-filled room.

As for the charge of ineffectiveness, Dista has a perfectly good case. It beggars the imagination to suppose that medical practitioners have been gulled or suborned into prescribing so expensively and extensively a medicament that works no better than an over-the-counter pill. Still, since experts on these matters are entitled to their adverse opinions, it does a criticized company no good at all, if a paper faithfully reprints the opinions, to, say, cancel its advertising. That time-dishonoured routine inevitably looks like intimidation and is an especially pernicious form of lie: suppressing the message or trying to, not because it is a false report, but because you don't like it.

The only way to demonstrate truth is by open, frontal assault on the critics – not on those who are merely messengers bearing the bad

146

news. If the news really is disastrous, the classic response is surely that mentioned earlier of Johnson & Johnson with its best-selling Tylenol – another pain-killer (it was open season on these in 1982). It wouldn't have done any good for that company to argue (rightly) that only a minute proportion of the capsules on sale had been tampered with by a homicidal maniac. The management took the disaster on the chin and withdrew the entire supply of Tylenol (which, funnily enough, is paracetamol).

The product has since gone back on sale in safer packaging, under the same brand name, and with a huge advertising budget. At a horrible cost of $100 million the company has emerged from its trauma with a strong position in the market and with an enhanced reputation – but no better luck. Its Zomax (yes, also a pain-killer), after five deaths, had to be withdrawn permanently – initial cost, $20 million. Misfortune aside, the lesson stands: when trouble strikes, any policy other than full, frank, and fair disclosure risks putting future markets at greater hazard than present ones. When trouble isn't striking, the lesson is no different.

Heller's Golden Rules

HOW TO . . .

. . . RUN RETAILING
1: In retailing, always develop a central, individual drive
2: Deserve a reputation for being True: Trustworthy, Recognized Unique, Efficient
3: Find out what kind of shop you're running – and run it accordingly

. . . USE ADVERTISING
1: Insist that your advertising works in the market place – not just in the agency's mind
2: Aim to shift brand preference in your favour
3: Seek to break the advertising mould – without breaking the rules

. . . AVOID POLITICS
1: Don't rely on protectionism – protect yourself
2: Don't market by using your muscles – unless forced

3: Don't use dirty tricks – they may cost more clean money than you think·

. . . DEFEND THE COMPANY
1: If you change the name, make sure you change the things that matter more
2: Integrate, modernize, spread and diversify – or else
3: Look after the market, and the name will look after itself

. . . USE PUBLICITY
1: Make the public believe in the product – not yourself
2: In PR, marry the words to the music: i.e., the truth to the reality
3: When trouble strikes (and when it doesn't) go for full and frank disclosure

SECTION FIVE
DIVERSITY

1: Damn La Différence

Anyone can see that a multi-market company is inherently stronger than a single-market one; provided, that is, that the multiple markets are all strong. If the only result of diversification is to lose on the swings what you gain on the roundabouts, that provides stability, true. But the steady state isn't the object of business enterprise – especially in markets where competition cannot be beaten lying down.

Worse still, many companies, great and small, were forced in the late 1970s to recognize that their bold forays into new markets, by product or geography, had produced so much loss on the swings that the profitable roundabouts were revolving to less than no ultimate effect. The resulting wave of retrenchment might lead one to speak of a new spirit being abroad in world business – although in one of the cases of withdrawal, 'abroad' somewhat misses the point. The case is Gulf Oil's retreat from making petrochemicals in Europe. The invasion of the supposedly rich and growing Continent by the US chemical giants was one of the more striking examples of the famed American Challenge of the 1960s – so why was the new spirit abroad taking Gulf, as it were, back home?

A case from a quite different industry provides the answer. In mid-1981 Philip Morris bought a 22 per cent stake in Rothmans International (a \$350 million puff) because it was dissatisfied with the results of its own diversification away from cigarettes. That bald announcement should have made any marketing professor swallow his Miller High Life beer down the wrong way – that brand being the key to a saga unsurpassed by any company diversifying into any business.

Using the marketing techniques it had refined with cigarette

150

brands, led by Marlboro, Philip Morris expanded Miller's beer sales by 20 per cent to 30 per cent per annum, elevated it from seventh to second place in the industry, shook up the entire brewing industry from top to bottom by its success, and invented the whole low-calorie beer sector. Triumph could hardly have been more spectacular – so what was the trouble? The Philip Morris complaint was that, like Gulf's chemicals in Europe, the marketing game hadn't been worth the financial candle.

In the previous four years Miller's beer assets had only yielded two percentage points more than one-month Treasury bills. With 30 per cent of the group's total sales, Miller produced only 11 per cent of operating income. At that, it did better than the company's 1978 purchase, Seven Up, which cost $515 million and wasn't making a cent: though even that improves greatly on Gulf's £10 million losses on £300 million of European turnover. Small wonder that Gulf cancelled its £100 million expansion project in Rotterdam, and thus undermined the business of its existing plants in the one-time wonder Euromarket.

The Morris and Gulf cases differ in that Gulf made a basic strategic error (in hindsight), while the impact of Miller on the market must have gone more than according to plan. Seven Up in turn was given the full Miller treatment (sales force trebled, production capacity upped, prices raised, trademark and packaging revamped, massive new advertising). But all such endeavours, like Gulf's in Europe, raise the ante horrendously. Buying markets at the price of negative or inadequate returns in capital never makes any sense.

What Motivates Mega-Deals

Even mighty purchasers like US Steel, Du Pont and Occidental have ended up, after their billion-dollar oil buys, enmeshed in selling assets to reduce gigantic debts. But was economic motivation actually the force behind the mega-deals? Does that explain, say, the US mergers between Dart and Kraft, or Nabisco and Standard Brands? Dart and Kraft (which sounds like another pair of reindeer for Santa Claus) was formed by merger in the autumn of 1980. Kraft is familiar worldwide from those invincibly processed slices of cheese. But Dart presents a real puzzle for food marketing experts. Who are they?

The answer is that they are, among other things, Tupperware and

151

Duracell batteries. Now Tupperware is more likely to contain comestibles than anything else: but you can neither nibble, chew, nor digest a battery. Which only rubs in the point that, these days, a food company is most unlikely to confine itself to the gullet. After all, only £6.7 billion of Unilever's £14.1 billion sales were in human food in 1982 – although this figure still exceeded total sales for the second largest food firm, the virtually all-pure Nestlé.

Once upon a time food was food, and non-food was non-food, and never the twain did meet. But just as non-food companies, like the Imperial Group, have moved into foods (on the simple thesis that, people have to eat), so food firms (like Borden, say) have moved into non-foods, because that delicious propensity to eat doesn't seem a good enough guarantee of the corporate future. To quote the *Financial Times*, 'In the mature food markets of the West the overall volume growth for food has become virtually static, which therefore encourages rationalisation of processing facilities.'

Glossing over the fact that 'virtually static growth' seems to be a contradiction in terms, the amalgamations of Dart and Kraft, or Nabisco and Standard, can hardly rationalize anything at all, since the product overlaps are few or non-existent. So what did motivate the respective managements to merge? The probability is that running a $5.9 billion Nabisco-Standard combine as Nabisco Brands simply feels more comfortable than living lower down the big leagues: especially shortly after your old enemy, Kraft, has just jumped to the top by kraftily absorbing Dart.

The old line in prize-fighting is 'The bigger they are, the harder they fall.' In Big Food, apparently, the argument is, the bigger they are, the harder it is for them to fall. It's that same argument of stability all over again. In the case of Dart and Kraft, moreover, that's what seems to have been achieved in the decade to 1982. In earnings per share and total return to shareholders, the company was stuck exactly in the middle of *Fortune*'s annual ranking of the 500 largest US industries – and so was the merged Nabisco Brands. Of course, the supposed and expected benefits of the mergers had yet to flow. But that depended on the managements bucking one of the most basic propositions in business: that managing diversity is a business in itself – and one of the toughest tasks in management.

The Sum of the Parts

Anybody who doesn't believe that should harken to these words. 'It is a very dangerous way to build a company – scary, too. It is logical that top management cannot sit in an office and build a company that way.' John H. Bryan, Jr, chairman and chief executive of Consolidated Foods, was speaking about his own company, which in 1974, to quote John Thackray in *Management Today*, 'was no less than 125 different businesses, and its $2,500 million-worth of sales all sprang from independent divisional fiefdoms which cared naught for headquarters direction from a scant staff of just 45'.

The divisional bosses were predominantly self-made men who had sold their businesses to Consolidated without relinquishing a shred of personal power. Bryan's family meat processing business had the same character and origin, but he was subsequently forced to launch a mighty effort to reshape Consolidated into something more akin to Procter & Gamble, a unified corporation expert in making and marketing fast-moving packaged goods.

This entailed getting rid of something like sixty businesses – in things like toy trains, curtain rods, men's shirts, women's clothing, and furniture. But disappearing unconsidered trifles like these is not the answer to the problems of diversified management. It can only build successfully round 'core' business: divisions that, paradoxically, are strong enough to stand on their own in markets which they dominate and which are worth dominating. Bryan simply didn't have enough of these – so he bought two, one of which, Hanes, is a fully-fashioned illustration of the point.

The business makes women's and men's hosiery and underwear, with $100 million in annual operating profits: half what Bryan paid for the entire company in 1977. The key products are L'eggs tights. Sold from store racks in egg-shaped containers, L'eggs propelled the company into the top position as a mass marketer of hosiery. The packaging, the promotion, and the merchandising (the stockings are sold like paperbacks, with Hanes filling racks at no cost or risk to the retailers) were brilliantly innovative, and rocketed Hanes right away from direct competition with the encroaching cheap private labels. In a trice L'eggs had half the market in supermarkets, drug stores, and discount stores – a market which it proceeded to segment carefully into support tights, high-fashion items and heavier-knit winter wear.

153

Bryan is proud of efforts to achieve similar breakthroughs with Sarah Lee (frozen croissants, now, as well as cakes,) and the Capri Sun soft-drink-in-a-pouch idea imported from Germany; less proud of the flop of L'eggs-style cosmetics. But the efforts emphasize that paradoxical task of the diversified corporation: it can only rise on the undiversified success of significant units.

Their success, in turn, can only be built by:

1. Product innovation aimed at finding gaps in the market or opening up new market areas.

2. Finding gaps in the distribution system peculiar to their markets, and sending the innovative product into the gaps (Bryan's soft-drink business, for instance, undercuts the market leaders by shipping, not to retail outlets, but direct to retailers' warehouses).

In other words, success depends overwhelmingly on skills and strategies which (unlike the principles of the national advertising that must support them) are intrinsic to the parts, not to the corporate whole.

For all Bryan's efforts, Consolidated's six main distinct activities, though now accounting for 93 per cent of sales, could hardly be much further apart without completely destroying any semblance of rationale for the company: frozen bakery products, processed meats, coffee (European mostly), soft drinks, hosiery and door-to-door vacuum cleaners. Bryan complained to Thackray that the same kind of criticism can be levelled at Procter & Gamble – which is in peanut butter, nappies, health care products, coffee, etc. – or any other big packaged goods company. So it can: that's why Wall Street has 'a clear view that companies like us have parts which are worth more than the whole corporation . . . which implies that we as managers of a big diversified company bring nothing to the sum of the parts'.

Of course, they do. But can they bring enough? Another of Thackray's interviewees in *Management Today* may well have the answer to the conundrum. 'A manager has got to know an industry intimately; to know and adjust to its mentality – it is amazing the variety of mentalities in different industries. You can't come in from the outside and hope to get that last 5 per cent.' The percentage to which the speaker, Richard M. Ringoen, refers is what results when you squeeze the last ounce of profit from the humdrum activities in which his company, Ball Corporation, earns its remarkable results.

Even Ringoen is 'just amazed at how well we do in some of the mundane businesses we're in. Because of this, we find the managers don't want to leave and go somewhere else in the company. They have their customers. They know the technology. What they want is to stick with it for ever.' The mundane businesses are in dreary, sometimes disaster areas like metal and glass containers, and zinc and plastic fabrication – in most of which Ball doesn't even have significant market shares: nothing like the fifth of the hosiery market won by L'eggs, for instance. It does get up to 15 per cent in glass jars for food: but in the two–piece beer and beverage can market, the figure is only 8–9 per cent. So how does Ball succeed?

First, its market-imbued managers concentrate on carefully selected niches: second, they are obsessed with achieving the lowest possible costs by the highest possible technology. In commodity markets like Ball's, as one analyst remarks, 'Manufacturers can't control prices. So they must control costs. The low–cost producer is the king of this business.' These two principles have carried Ball through recession and industrial shake-ups with far more success than competitors who have sought to diversify heavily away from packaging and containers: American Can into financial services, Continental into gas and oil, Owens-Illinois into hospital management. 'When you talk with most corporate managements, the conventional wisdom you hear is that a company should have a balanced portfolio of investments with countervailing cyclicalities,' says Thomas B. Clark, director of corporate planning. But Ball 'found that it just wasn't true. The probability of being able to do this is minimal.'

In other words, Ball manages what is actually a fair degree of diversity by *not* acting like managers of diversity: another paradox, which Ringoen can explain. He treats all the business lines with an even strategic hand because 'I hate to see companies that allocate priorities and express preferences about their different lines of business and say, "This one is a cash cow, and that one a star". Theoretically, we could squeeze all the cash out of the glass business and then plough it into high-technology defence areas – meanwhile telling the different management teams different things.' But 'you don't get the best results that way. It could be devastating for the motivation of young guys in glass. We want to treat them all alike, and expect each to do his best.'

What does Ball's centre do? It searches constantly for ways in which the individual businesses can better serve their markets and run themselves. In 1978, for instance, Ball bought a plastic injection moulding plant that was far more profitable than its own troubled business. Why? 'We got the founders, who were two brothers, to sit down and define their principles of operation: something they'd never done.' Among the principles which they wrote down were a high level of automation, operating-room cleanliness, no secondary operations, and small productive units. That opened Ringoen's eyes to a principle of his own: make divisional bosses work out their own principles, and stick to them. In beverage containers, for instance, Ball's principles say it will make only 9- and 16-ounce cans, two sizes that together have 80 per cent of the US beverage can market. 'Every month, somewhere in the country somebody comes to our people with an idea for making a different size can – say a 7-ounce can for the wine market – but they know to tell them "no",' according to Ringoen. 'If the divisions manage within those self-imposed constraints they'll be left pretty much alone,' notes Clark.

Follow that kind of approach, and managing and marketing, even with businesses that vary far more widely than Ball's, become far easier and far more effective. The logic of diversification is ultimately the same as that of concentration. Bad businesses obey Gresham's Law and drive out good ones. The multi-form firm really needs to be managed like a product portfolio – in which no product is allowed ascendancy in the top managerial mind, but every product, as at Ball, gets the concentrated attention of the managements who actually have it in their ever-loving care.

2: Mergers Make Strange Managers

You shouldn't always believe what companies say, even if the words have the effect of pillorying them. For instance, Roberto Goizueta, promoted in a spectacular personal leap to revitalize Coca-Cola, promptly ran into heavy flak for bottling up Columbia Pictures with a $765 million bid. What, the Wall Street critics wanted to know, did peddling pop have in common with films like *Annie*, Columbia's $40 million musical?

The true answer is nothing at all – except that Old King Coke reckons to know a thing or three about marketing, especially promotion and merchandising, a field in which, by comparison, movie men are babes unborn. At least, that was one of the arguments adduced by Goizueta. But the analogy between promoting people into cinemas and into pop bottles doesn't bear much examination; films are essentially one-offs, and the universal, all but unbeatable, Coke franchise is based on continuity and repetition.

The salient fact, though, is that even Coke is not ultimately unbeatable. The reason why Goizueta, new broom and all, won his promotion was that Pepsi-Cola had been fizzing all too fast for the peace of the royally rich clique of Atlanta businessmen who are Coca-Cola's time-lords. Just like Jacques Bergerac, plucked from ITT by the legendary Charles Revson to run Revlon, the new Coke boss plainly saw that one quick route to financial targets (growing faster than inflation in Coke's case) is to buy that growth.

Funnily enough, Revlon did precisely that in one field, health care, which Goizueta examined and found wanting (maybe rightly, given Revlon's lacklustre recent record). Why? Because it involved high technology – and that was one of Goizueta's diversification no-nos,

157

along with high capital investment in plant and inability to grow rapidly without dramatic increase in market share. That last stipulation, obviously enough, would rule out Coke itself. After all those years of massive consumer bombardment, its chances of fast outgrowing the whole soft drinks market are hardly high. It's a problem that eventually comes to all successful firms, even on far smaller stages: when you and the market have matured, what next? The movie market, of course, is even more aged in the wood than Coke's: the behaviour of audience statistics round the world has been as discouraging as the failure rate of feature films is sobering. Anyway, as Goizueta pointed out in his own defence, Columbia is only a tenth of Coca-Cola's size: which means that it can hardly make a mighty difference to the Atlanta giant's performance.

No: the drinks market was where Goizueta's cause had to be won or lost. The real reason for the Columbia buy was to provide a rich cash flow that would underpin the greatest shake-up the US soft drinks empire had ever seen: distributor reorganization and executive revivalism went hand-in-hand with an unprecedented flow of new product launches, in which Diet Coke sprang out of nowhere to beat all-comers in its sector: including Coke's own Tab. The purpose of diversification must always be to add strength to the basic business, never to dilute the drink. As Goizueta's new ad slogan rightly said, 'Coke is it!' The basic business always is.

The Perils of Purchase

Why Goizueta succeeded is made perfectly clear by why others failed. 'The bottom line in ten big mergers' ran the headline in a 1982 issue of *Fortune* magazine. Good or bad news for the whale-sized corporations which are still so avidly swallowing the smaller fry? Alas, for all the experience that should have been garnered in three decades of unexampled amalgamation, the thumbs still turn down – even though half the cases actually did have better 1981 earnings per share than they would hypothetically have made without their 1971 acquisition.

In four of the cases, the acquiring managements could say, hands on hearts, that the buy and its consequences were genuinely good. But even in two of the four, less encouraging notes are sounded. Drug firm Squibb, which in 1971 couldn't even 'spell out' the wondrous 'growth opportunities' that lay ahead of the Lanvin-Charles of the Ritz cosmetics business (a $206 million buy), admitted, 'We made some mistakes because we didn't understand the business.' Another drug firm, American Cyanamid, also went into cosmetics, with Shulton (for $106 million), and confessed that 'synergy in research took too long to come'. Funnily enough, relative failures said much the same – as in: 'We made our share of mistakes; we took too long to move down the learning curve.'

That was Heublein, the brewers, talking about Kentucky Fried Chicken ($237 million). Then, take a drug-maker treading the same route as Squibb and Cyanamid into cosmetics, etc.: Schering. It found that its 'international people didn't adapt well to consumer products. That synergism took longer than we thought.' Its $644 million purchase of Plough knocked 19 per cent off hypothetical 1981 earnings. Plough was the most expensive of the ten buys – both absolutely and as a percentage of the purchaser's book value (815 per cent, no less). But expense, absolute or relative, has no visible correlation with success or failure. Nor does closeness of fit with the acquirer's own business.

Thus drugs and toiletries don't sound impossibly far apart – but only look at Schering. The answer, which is no surprise, lies in management, in the speed and the skill which the acquirer applies, or makes sure is applied, in its new market. Even so, the task of managing unfamiliar markets brings no bonanzas. Relating net profits in 1981 dollars to the purchase price in good old 1971 bucks gives yield figures for the four successes ranging from 7 per cent to 13 per cent.

Merely think of what those 1971 purchase prices were really worth in buying power ten years later, and the old lesson is doubled or redoubled. A purchasing company is buying one of the toughest management tasks, as four of the ten proved in the hardest possible way. Three of the businesses they bought in 1971 had been sold, with one more allegedly up for grabs. If you can't manage 'em, sell 'em, is a sensible policy; but it is, of course, an admission of failure. The failures, note, were not failures of the acquired companies, but of the acquiring managements.

That diagnosis is made clear by studying the many large, merged failures formed out of competitors. Post mortem analysis usually reveals that the union was never properly consummated for years after the parties formally became one. The problem wasn't that of managing diversity (the problem which lays low most major

159

companies which try to buy their way into new markets); rather, the problem is one of managing *tout court* – of imposing the common direction, common controls, and common sense which any operation needs.

That explains why multi-millionaire financiers often batten even richer from ventures of baffling diversity without ever leaving their luxurious pads for some lugubrious office. They know what they own, they know what they want, and they know what to do if they don't get it: they shoot the pianist. The businesses stay firmly rooted in their own markets, and the authoritarian drive motivates their managers.

Take the career of Sir Maxwell Joseph. His passing removed a man who, on the record, must have been one of the great originals in marketing. Yet he wasn't a shopkeeper, like the late Sir Jack Cohen of Tesco; he wasn't a caterer, like Lord Forte; and he wasn't a hotelier, milkman, or brewer, either. All the same, he ended up with an extraordinarily varied and rich marketing portfolio – beer, wine and spirits, food, restaurants, cigarettes, milk, retailing, industrial catering, hotels worldwide, etc; all brought (or bought) together amazingly fast.

If there was nothing else to it, Joseph could be discussed as just another conglomerating financier. The hallmark of that breed, however, is often that very inability to exploit the accumulated enterprises which laid *Fortune*'s unlucky acquirers low. But under the Joseph aegis the Eden Vale arm of Express Dairy, for one example, chalked up some notable new products. While few of the Joseph enterprises are famed far and wide for marketing excellence, their worst days and mistakes mostly predated the Master: the Watney's Red beer fiasco, for example, was all Watney's own.

By and large, Grand Metropolitan operations easily survive critical scrutiny – including that of customers who are overwhelmingly located in the large-scale markets. But how could a man brought up in the wheel-and-deal, fat-cat world of property develop so competent a touch with the consuming masses? One answer is that Joseph, even when confined to a handful of modest West End hotels (as he was so remarkably late as 1969), thought in straight marketing terms. Very early on, for instance, he appointed people to market his hotel rooms, then a rare activity in Britain.

When he broke out of the medium time, too, Joseph bought big:

while his deals could generally be justified in property terms, Joseph in fact went for significant consumer franchises, especially serving the richer South of England, and all in the high-cash-flow businesses needed to extract him from the high debt incurred by such costly purchases. Above all, Joseph demonstrated the truth that any marketing business consists of two things: the fixed assets, and the consumer franchise (which is also an asset). Of necessity, Joseph's approach (not to mention his own personality, which included a taste for conspicuously short working weeks) meant decentralized management of businesses that kept their separate market identity – and that is why they worked.

Conran's Happy Marriage

That same essential quality – knowing what you want and how to make others get it – explains how Sir Terence Conran overcame the problem of the enormous contrast in styles, though not in sector, embodied in the Habitat–Mothercare merger. Happily it wasn't a contrast of personalities, since Mothercare's Selim Zilkha, very wisely, bowed out of the shop door at once. The world of difference lay in the development and nature of the two organizations: one a large, £169.7 million retail chain, set up and built up in deliberate imitation of the Marks & Spencer model: the other a much smaller, specialist business, whose retail outlets seem to have developed from the merchandise.

Where Terence Conran had created his Habitat market as a brilliant taste-maker, Zilkha concentrated on cornering parts of the business already being done by other stores. Where Zilkha could initially draw on the family fortune to finance his early hard climb, Conran fought his way through his own vicissitudes with pluck and a great willingness to learn: it's typical that he agreed to a behind-the-boardroom-door TV programme on Habitat when its fortunes were being heavily battered.

Since those traumatic days Conran has seasoned his expansionism with heavy doses of prudence. Where Mothercare went for the US market in a big way, and earned big losses for its pains, Habitat proceeded step by step, keeping its down-side American risks as low as possible – and perhaps (who knows?) sacrificing some up-side potential as a result. The Conran strategy has been well judged for the purposes of a group that has evolved into a significant retailer specifically by shunning the mass market. Yet an overwhelming proportion of the merged companies' sales are a long way down from Habitat's original NW1 segment.

There was no immediate evidence from the past that the smaller company's management had either the down-market or the up-management skills that were required. But Conran and Co., by prudently applying what lessons of their past were relevant, and learning some new tricks fast, succeeded in rapidly establishing the combined viability of their disparate chain. Where Mothercare had doubled its turnover since 1978, while net profits had only risen by a fifth, Conran's management elevated the business's performance on all measures with what looked like surprising ease.

Pre-tax profits up by 90 per cent on a turnover rise of just over half gave early, convincing evidence that the new Mothercare was working. The principles were simple: change through consultation, not dictate: refitting all shops with a new colour scheme; uplifting the quality and image of the products. The Conran team drew on its experience both in the Habitat retail operation and as designer for other retailers to do the simple and obvious well and smoothly.

The simple and the obvious are highlighted by a banal, but true, observation from Conran – 'If people are offered well-designed, well-made products at a sensible price, they will like and buy them'; and by another commonplace from John Stephenson, the director who masterminded the Mothercare operation. 'I've been asked when Mothercare will be finished. That's a stupid question: it has to be a continuing process of evaluation and change.' In that process, obvious or not, the £110 million price paid for Mothercare began to seem perfectly reasonable – because of perfectly reasonable management.

In the beginning and the end, the purchase of another business, diversified or complementary, is just another commercial venture, no different from a new factory or new product, in that its justification depends on the planning, the cost, the execution and the results – in that inevitable order. Ignore the marketplace realities, allow a gap to emerge and grow between that real-life potential and the actual costs, and you get a disaster – which you richly deserve.

3: The Discontinuous Present

Do today's corporate essentials represent a break in continuity? Has management in general, and marketing in particular, been changed radically by the brave new markets? According to an article in *Fortune*, the answer is a resounding Yea. It quotes one academic to the effect that 'All of a sudden, industrial products are like Hula Hoops.' Without a doubt, the pace of markets has hotted up to relative frenzy; product life cycles have shortened by as much as a third; product innovations follow hard on each other's heels; no price structure is safe.

All very true: but more important by far than events is how management reacts to them. In the reactions described by the magazine, the starting point is that everywhere the customer is king. One man at Hewlett-Packard told *Fortune* that 'we'd never heard of' focus groups. But once they had, getting a bunch of computer purchasers to talk proved invaluable – surprise, surprise. Over at Texas Instruments, the example cited is the $660 million collapse in home computers, blamed on inadequate observance of the marketing injunction, Know Your Competitor: when it launched a price war, TI just didn't know that Commodore's costs were decisively lower.

Lesson Three is Know the Man Next Door. You can no longer afford to let design, manufacturing, and marketing operate as separate, sometimes warring factions, especially when it comes to innovation. In a move led by IBM, companies are thus even putting design and manufacture under combined command. Speed is the fourth necessity: speed in development, speed into the marketplace. You can get it more easily by simply stopping engineers making the big changes they love *after* the initial process of market identification and product design is complete.

Fifth, and obviously vital at a time of fast change, cannibalize, even supersede your own miracle before some other swine does. If necessary, join the other swine – form joint ventures (as AT&T has with Olivetti, say) rather than go it alone, however rich you are in money and technology.

Through all these five points there runs a note of impending, if not onrushing doom, an 'or else' based on the hard facts of rapid corporate disaster in the naked markets. In the light of actual events, nobody could accuse *Fortune* of scare-mongering. Indeed, beware of being Mattelled or Warnered is a warning that should be engraved deep on the hearts of the new entrepreneurial companies. Few firms have ever expanded so explosively as Mattel, whose electronic games doubled to $556 million in a single year: and Warner's Atari division multiplied its sales ten times in five years to an incredible $2 billion. Yet both crashed into horrendous losses – and the warning is that the calamities were not beyond control.

Indeed, control is the key word. Rapid growth of highly profitable business (Mattel had $67 million of electronic earnings in 1982–3) customarily covers up a multitude of sins. Though Mattel won its rapid success by leapfrogging Atari, it then failed to upgrade its game player; missed out on video game cartridges; and came to market with a $150 computer, $50 dearer than the competition. Exit computer. Exit Mattel, back to toys, out of electronics altogether.

Where the toy company failed was in not building up management to control and match the explosive electronic growth. At Atari, lack of control showed most conspicuously as disorganization: a dozen separate un-coordinated divisions, according to *Time* magazine, with forty-nine scattered buildings, five finance departments, terrible overlaps, no pay structure, too many products, and too many people (now cut from 9,800 to 3,500). Apple showed much the same syndrome – its Macintosh white hope, for one example, was produced independently from and without any reference to the Lisa computer, which uses identical technology.

Explosive-growth companies need to be reminded that they are mortal, and that the management basics which they blithely ignore in boom time will be desperately needed when market conditions change – as change they will. What makes the Atari and Mattel horror stories so striking is the speed and severity of change, as the bottom dropped out of games and home computer markets and prices: Mattel's Intellivision in 1984 was fetching a sixth of its 1982 price, while the

Sinclair computer, under the Timex name, was selling at the same time at pocket calculator levels. Small wonder that Timex, itself the victim of poor control, had to follow Texas Instruments, Mattel, and others out of the US computer market. The pace of change in markets is so fast today that even growth companies have little time to repair their basic deficiencies – after, that is, those errors have found them out.

Mark the Market

Nor is it only the growth companies. In an industry mature to the point of grey hairs, BAT lost enormous face for a group of such size (£11.5 billion in sales) and sophistication by losing £53 million on its UK cigarette trade, ignominiously halved by a semi-pullout in early 1984. This isn't, after all, a trade where management knew naught. True, the lush learning curve up which BAT's tobacco profits had risen didn't apply to the UK, thanks to the time-dishonoured carve-up which kept Imperial Tobacco out of overseas markets, and BAT exclusively in them. Over the post-war years, this separation from home built up into the strong frustration among BAT managers who, flushed with success abroad, were sure they could burn Imps badly in Britain.

Their subsequent five-year failure to catch fire has three possible causes. Either the BATmen were not so white-hot at marketing as they thought; or they simply made a hash (which happens to the hottest of marketers at least once in their lives); or anybody would have burnt out against the dark background of a 25 per cent fall in smoking. It's churlish, though inevitable, to say that market research should have given some warning of the latter collapse. But all factors, the unavoidable and the voluntary alike, played a part; not only was it impossible to out-market Imps, but BAT's chosen strategy, excessive promotion in support of none-too-brilliant brands, was unwise.

The BAT brands had no strong selling proposition, unique or otherwise. Spending couldn't make up the deficiency – given that full frontal assault hardly ever succeeds without a three-to-one advantage in resources. BAT couldn't outspend and undercut Imps indefinitely. The lesson is that today a giant barging into a new market is subject to much the same limitations as a relative midget.

The unavoidable nature of these limitations – the fact that nobody can buck the market – emerges clearly from the ten-year growth

165

listing which *Management Today* published in March 1984. The rampant retailers stuck out a mile. Habitat-Mothercare, MFI, Burton, Superdrug and Comet were respectively third, fifth, sixth, seventh and ninth: a concentration which emphasizes not just that, these days, the shop is mightier than the workshop, but that the market is mightier than anybody.

The retail predominance alone is none too surprising in a Britain whose manufacturers have mostly long since given up, if not the ghost, at least any hope of growth on the strict conditions met so triumphantly by the ace retailers: a ten-year rise in earnings per share, after correction for inflation. On this all too real criterion, BAT suffered a decline exceeding 5 per cent annually, during a decade when Comet rocketed away by nearly 22 per cent per annum.

True, the famous five shot up from bases which, back in 1973–4, were knee-high, either because so was the company's stature, or because it was performing drearily in the Sagging Seventies: like Burton. However, the retail stardom also has a highest common factor. Each in its own way, the wonder-chains won by identifying new market trends and smartly adapting strategies and products to match. Michael Hollingbery, who built up Comet from a single inherited shop in Hull, is explicit on the subject.

Observing (simply enough) that the death of retail price maintenance meant the birth of cut-price retailing, and that the pervasive car made possible purveying out of town, he moved swiftly because (as he told *Management Today*), 'I was frightened that if we didn't do it, Tesco would.' (The fact that Tesco didn't may partly explain why it ranked seventy-nine places below Comet, with a negative figure for growth in earnings per share.) Differentiate, specialize, segment – and do it all with speed and conviction: that formula for retail riches has an oddly familiar ring.

It's precisely the policy which the pundits have been trying to force down the throats of manufacturing industry – along with the warning (also voiced by Hollingbery) to 'give the customer what he wants, or go broke'. What explains the dearth of successful British firms supplying the things that the gee-whiz retailers sell? In case after case, the thing-makers allowed their strategies to be shaped by what they made, rather than by what could be marketed profitably.

That is nothing but the oldest of business basics. Hark back, too, to that list of the new management necessities as established by *Fortune*.

Any old marketing hand should experience a sense, not of brave new management, but of *déjà vu*. Isn't this what marketing has always been about? Keeping close to the customer, watching the competition like an especially famished hawk, bringing the functions together on co-ordinated product development, getting products through development at maximum speed, beating competition to the punch: these are among the oldest rules of the game. They have also, true, been honoured more in the breach than in the observance. But there is something new under the sun: the fact that, because of the newly ferocious pace, rule-breakers may expect (like TI, BAT in British smokes, Atari and Mattel) to get broken – and that right soon.

Triumph in Turbulence

'Turbulence' is the word used by Bill Ramsay, director of development of General Foods in the UK, to describe these conditions in world markets. He pointed out, in a paper on brand marketing, that the world economy had gone from growth through crisis to flatness; that brand marketing had passed from proliferation through rationalization to polarization; that consumer requirements had moved from choice to price/value to identity; that the source of profit, market expansion in the sixties, became margin improvement in the next decade: now it is winning the battle for market share. This all means that management has had to switch its attention from diversification through resource allocation to competitive strategy – which is where this chapter began, with the huge competitive pressure being felt by US companies and its consequences for management.

Ramsay's conclusions on what these consequences are for brand marketing were emphatic.

1. Recognize that the brand is in a state of flux and transition. The conditions of the sixties have disappeared for ever. Anticipate the changes to come.

2. Build a strategic view of your brand adjusted to the new realities. Learn and relearn the key leverages that affect the market you are in. Look for segmentation opportunities. Think how you would enter your market if you were a new competitor.

3. Analyze your consumers. They are no longer conformist and uncomplicated. The role of women is changing. They are smarter, less predictable.

4. The manufacturer and the trade are strategically interdependent. Each needs the other. The manufacturer needs a detailed trade marketing plan, the trade needs a brand marketing plan.

5. Invest heavily in advertising when you have a new brand, a new item or a genuinely improved product (or service).

6. Use research and development to improve or at least maintain your competitive quality.

7. Accept innovation as a necessity for your category and organize accordingly. New products need to be technologically driven as well as market driven.

Once again the wisdom is ancient, but the urgency is new – and powerful. Ramsay quoted from a *Harvard Business Review* article a passage that should be engraved on the marketing mind. 'The key to long-term success – even survival – is what it has always been: to invest, to innovate, to create value. Such determination, such striving to excel requires leaders.' So there *is* strong continuity: the difference is that the lessons of what has always been true have to be observed in a setting so strongly discontinuous that what is old can look frighteningly new.

4: If You Can't Beat 'Em, Get Beaten

The great European takeover surge in the US can be looked at from many different angles. But they mostly give a similar view: that of the relative loss of power of many giant US corporations. The loss has been considerably redressed by the strong Reagan economic recovery, but the fall from grace was still substantial. Nor was it merely financial: the relative marketing failure has been on a vast scale – so vast that the astonishing has become the commonplace.

In a single week of spring 1982, for instance, a huge British conglomerate bought one of the most famous names in US retailing, while a British advertising agency, of modest size internationally, became positively immodest by purchasing a far larger American firm. Not so many years ago the idea of BAT paying $310 million for Marshall Field, or the Saatchis pocketing Compton, for a $29.2 million down payment, would have bordered on the unthinkable. Now nobody turns a hair – although these deals symbolize one of the most extreme turnabouts of modern times.

America is still the world's leading marketplace, the largest by far, the most varied, the most competitive, the one most likely to innovate and to accept innovation – but no longer right across the board. In retailing, for instance, one-time leaders such as those taken over by BAT (Gimbels, Saks, and now the Chicago-based Marshall) steadily slipped through lack of the aggressive, enterprising management that created them in the first place. The decline of the once-great A&P (now headed by an Englishman) in supermarkets has also been stupefying to behold.

The universal spectacle has been that of Europeans using retailing techniques imported from the US to much greater effect than the originators. The process just described should sound familiar to followers of the Japanese miracle: in the major beleaguered industries (like cars, where the Americans have been so tortured by Toyota, *et al*), Western manufacturing mammoths have been similarly hoist with their own petards.

Invaders of the US have been exploiting not merely their own thrustfulness, but that long *rallentando* of much big US business. The same phenomenon has been seen in Britain, as the giants of the 1960s have lost touch with their markets, or stayed in the wrong markets, or relied on money rather than management to diversify away from their base troubles – only to find peripheral ones instead. From International Stores to Yardley, Wiggins Teape to Gimbels, the Marshall Field buyer, BAT, bought itself a peck of problems: hence the result – an 80 per cent rise in sales in five years, but only a 50 per cent gain in net profits, while tobacco, though reduced to half of the assets, still accounted for 72 per cent of trading profit.

Even before the Marshall buy, though, nearly half these profits came from North America. As these inexorable trends continue, more and more UK groups will find themselves with a British tail wagging a vast American dog. It will be an extreme test of their ability not just to manage, but to adapt, and to adapt to a shifting scene: for the big company economy is in flux, all over the world.

One of the most striking signs of change is the new currency being given to a management maxim of noble antiquity: 'If you can't beat 'em, join 'em.' The new twist which this is getting in the remarkable evolution of today's markets is the same in many different contexts, whether it's IBM buying into Intel's micro-circuitry, or VW teaming up with Renault to make an automatic gearbox, or Glaxo placing its US wonder-drug in the hands of Hoffmann-La Roche. Even the greatest of companies can't hope to cover the whole gamut of products and marketing requirements imposed by fast, specialized markets.

The old received idea was that the giant used its financial and marketing muscle to get mighty economies of scale. These days, the economist of scale has to cope with much greater variety; he needs far more flexibility than of yore; and scale costs too much for one company to manage all the scales on its own. Thus Renault and VW compete on body shells etc., but combine on automatic transmissions. Thus Glaxo and Hoffmann-La Roche race each other to the marketable patents – but the former decides that the latter's American marketing strength is worth more than its own patented exclusivity.

By similar tokens, IBM has perhaps the most powerful marketing image of any company in the closing decades of the century. But even in a relatively confined market like data processing even IBM lacks all the specialized expertise that moves the market. Hence it wisely turned to Intel, the archetypal Silicon Valley venture, for the vital innards of its sure-to-succeed (with its IBM label) Personal Computer. Hence, in turn, Intel, now dependent on IBM for huge chunks of business, found it advantageous to take in a senior partner – the 18 per cent IBM stake underwrites Intel's ability to go on satisfying the market, while Intel's micro-circuit skills should guarantee that IBM won't fall behind the Japanese.

Of course, cups have many a slip between themselves and lips. Maybe Intel would end up as a wholly-owned subsidiary of IBM: maybe Glaxo's deal with Roche would work out lamentably, as other such joint ventures have done. Whatever the risks, the principle was plainly right. Even the effective, high-growth specialist like Intel will come, sooner or later, to a point of no return – where, to guarantee its progress, it needs more marketing outlets and more money.

Preserving independence, though, is highly desirable. As always, the French have a word for it – or rather a few words: 'groupement d'intérêts économiques'. It's the legal term for a combination of parts which isn't a merger (with all the familiar disadvantages thereof), but a union. More and more, sensible firms will be seeking economies of scale in this way. For those that don't join 'em may very well be beaten.

From Random to Rah-Rah

Can the principle of 'grouping interests' be applied within the firm, though? The answer would appear to be 'No' if the question is asked of a company like Vickers, one of those companies that seem to be born (or reborn) unlucky. For years, every step forward by the one-time armaments giant seemed to have been followed by at least half a step back. Before the 1983 dividend-cutting plunge of a third, the company's earnings per share had declined in a decade by 7.8 per cent annually – according to *Management Today*'s inflation-corrected earnings per share league. Yet in the early 1970s (and again in 1980, when the Rolls-Royce Motors merger took place) Vickers, not for the first time, had promised to come right.

Maybe so long a run of bad luck – with the American setback on the car side the blow of the early 1980s – is too long to be attributed to the fates alone. Look at it this way: what do luxury cars, lithographic plates, health care, and bottling machinery have in common? The only answer is that Vickers was in all these markets in 1983. In fact, its interests were grouped in about eleven diverse main activities, which in 1982 showed the following pattern – profits up, five; profits down, five; unchanged, one.

No doubt even an infant statistician would spot this as a typical random pattern. The randomness is typical of this kind of conglomerate – held together not by any marketing unity, but mostly by the weak cement of history. The biggest constituents of Vickers, the world's most famous luxury cars, account for only 19 per cent of sales. The group just doesn't have the market base which helped BOC (also once seemingly luckless) to change its luck. But even in 1982–3 BOC's traditional core in gases, etc. accounted for 48 per cent of sales and 80 per cent of operating profit. Very typically, one part of all activity accounts for the lion's share of all useful results.

That was true of Rolls-Royce cars in 1981, when they turned in 38 per cent of group profits. But those motors needed to generate at least double the sales to give Vickers the bread-and-butter single-market base required by every diversified business; except those conglomerates which are masterminded by the corporate jugglers whose equals the Vickers management wouldn't pretend to be. The Vickers men aren't jugglers at all, but their strategy and control had to spread over a dozen different businesses – and more: a feeble nothing of profit came from £49.6 million of 'activities each with under £15 million sales in 1982'. 'Activities each with' are no answer at all – to anything. Rather, they prove that a management hasn't grasped the fundamental necessity of answering two questions. Do you know what you're doing? And are you doing it properly?

No less a company than ICI came to the conclusion that it couldn't give an honest 'Yes' to questions of this variety. Its retreat from its Millbank fortress to a far smaller London head office is a landmark in the history of Big Business. Indeed, 'big' is an operative word: small has become fashionably beautiful, and ICI has always had a penchant for following management modes – raising its hemline rather late, but with enthusiasm.

172

Its new organizational rah-rah, though, reflects more than modishness. For that matter, so does the whole worldwide reaction away from the centralized mammoths which once dominated the industrial scene – those 300 which, in one popular scenario, would have been ruling the international roost by now. No doubt the 300 would have included, on any reasonable projection, the near-bankrupts International Harvester and Massey-Ferguson. Size has been no protection against the intensified, segmented competition which now really rules, and which demands companies organized round the sharp, marketing end.

Certain businesses, though, will never be good again in our lifetimes, or in anybody's lives. Steel is already a shadow of its former self. In ICI's business, many bulk chemicals hold out the same sad prospect of eternal over-supply and low returns, yet at such large volumes that few managements have yet dared to shed what is in fact the base-load of their corporations. What they can shed, though, is the base-load of management: the fungus-like growth of second-guessers and satellites which multiplied in the days when size dominated.

ICI carried this to an unusually baffling extent, because the real power of command over men and resources always lay with its mighty divisions. The efforts of the executive directors to execute, given this essential powerlessness, were cramped. The millstone in the HQ's nickname of Millstone House must have weighed especially heavily round the necks of some of its own higher inhabitants. Pity the poor director impossibly responsible at one and the same time for a function, a geographical area, and a division.

The alternative method of management, by performance, is now well established as faster and far more effective, with a small centre exacting and monitoring results from separate, market-oriented operations headed by individual chief executives, and with the growth markets separated out and properly, profitably exploited. But the retreat from Millstone House would have failed if it had been merely organizational. The force that drives the engine is all-important, and that force can only be marketing.

Colonel Urwick's Wheel

That being so true, and so obvious, how on earth is it that the marketing concept has failed to penetrate all managerial minds? As noted in an earlier chapter, Col. Lyndall F. Urwick expounded the concept a whole half-century back. He warned that 'The main job of distribution is not to get rid of what production makes, it is to tell production what it ought to make.' Splendid stuff, and obviously true. But set that 1933 quote against this 1984 one from *Business Week*, on Edwin H. Land, the founder of Polaroid:

> Land believed that success depended on coming up with innovative products, then persuading people to buy them, and in his day Polaroid used little or no market research. . . . By contrast, Land's successors are looking outward to the market. They are taking their cues from potential customers . . . and are tailoring their technology to meet the need, not the other way round.

The reason for this conversion was not the retirement of Land (though that helped), but the three years of declining sales which have turned Polaroid from *wunderkind* to has-been.

This great innovative company was not alone in ignoring market research: to take just one other example (the biggest you could find), so did General Motors. In describing that company's magnificent turnround, one of its top engineers was moved to remark that the company is now 'trying to find out what the customers want'. About time, too – but what explained a neglect so long and so grave that these mighty managements proved, by their awful results, how right Urwick was?

Nor can the question only be asked of US leaders. At the afore-mentioned ICI, in the darkest days of the Fibre Division's attempt to cut losses by cutting back, one move, incredibly, was to dismantle the marketing department; the new, far more promising strategy is marketing-led, using technology to develop special fibres that the end-user wants, and employing marketing razzmatazz to exploit these desires. Quote (from *Management Today*): 'The biggest fundamental thing we have done is to stand our business on its head and ask "What does the market need?", rather than produce the goods and tell the salesmen to go out and sell.'

There's Colonel Urwick's wheel being reinvented all over again – note, once more under the duress of desperately bad results. But strength can flow from weakness. It takes strong management for the company that was first, and famously so, into polyester filament yarn, to be first out: or (another example of ICI daring to dare) for the

174

company that invented polyethylene to abandon the product. Today's naked markets have stripped even giants of their clothes. Those prepared to re-dress themselves in the marketing concept, though, can truly hope to capitalize on the innate strength of both the company and the modern marketplace. Riches, as well as naked competition, lie in the market's variety. The riches can only be won by companies that can organize a varied and vital response to match.

5: The Necessity of Niche

The recession from which Britain and the world emerged as the eighties developed was in one respect the strangest in history – deep in its impact on production and employment, but shallow in its effect on consumption. Throughout the years of high and mounting unemployment, the world featured market after market whose buoyancy was evidence of plenty amidst dearth. The plenty is buying power: the dearth jobs of the traditional variety. If an article in *Fortune* is right (and it's very hard to refute), the phenomenon won't disappear with recovery – no matter how vigorous. As its headline says, 'The mass market is splitting apart.' Not only is the gap between rich and poor widening, visibly and substantially, but the middle class is also polarizing (meaning families with incomes of $15,000 to $35,000).

While the number of these solid citizens has fallen as a proportion of all families, the percentages earning above $35,000 or below $15,000 actually rose. The explanation isn't far to seek. Nearly all the new job creation in the US has been in services, while manufacturing's share of employment has fallen. Service jobs are mostly lower paid – except in the management and professional classes. Hence the $35,000-plus proliferation, the $15,000-minus increase, and the obvious conclusion for marketers – that the top money lies at the top end.

That plainly means going up-market, tapping the purses of the new class which can afford to change cars often, to gobble up home computers, and to buy increasingly expensive wines from its favourite supermarket. Indeed, Sainsbury has plainly achieved a not so minor miracle of positioning – preserving the mass market franchise which is vital to a national supermarket chain, while also establishing a rich pre-eminence as the upper-middle mart. That mart's suppliers have rosy

176

prospects in a Britain where US demographic changes are not only mirrored, but magnified – factory employment has fallen absolutely as well as relatively. *Fortune*'s parallel conclusion for those 'used to selling millions of their products to middle-income folks' thus looks highly relevant, too – their prospects are altogether darker.

For the smart retailer, though, the prospects could hardly be brighter. In Britain, as in America, super-growth has come to retailers exploiting the newer mass-marketing techniques of reaching the more affluent consumer. A decade ago Habitat, Comet, MFI, Harris Queensway, etc. were of relatively minor account in the retail stakes. But, in the age of the car and the selective purchaser, of onerous wage costs and omnipresent price sensitivity, the retailer with car access, or takeaway goods, or central, computerized warehousing, or cut prices, has a huge advantage over the traditional High Street retailer when cashing in on the demographic trends.

Main Street is no different. Toys 'R' Us, the US chain which created four of 1983's five highest paid Americans, specializes in off-loading toys in lavish quantities from warehouse-like premises, a technique being tailored to several trades, including computers. In the computer market, companies like IBM are now being brought face to face with the consumer for the first time, as products like the Personal Computer are pushed through dealers, rather than hawked by the company's own sales force.

In one degree or other, the same rethinking is now required practice for all comers hoping to sell through the new retail powers. They must build even more powerful consumer franchises to force the stocking of their offerings on the trade titans. In US computer retailing there are already fears that the strength of IBM, Apple and a very few others will drive out the smaller fry simply through lack of shelf space. In the economic society now emerging, not so much post-industrial as consumer-dominated, access to the consumer is increasingly critical. Most companies have no choice but to become consumer-dominated in step, a move which will take them a long way from their old industrial bases.

By the same token, the omens are awful for companies that haven't moved from that base – or won't. The sorry fact that Britain's trade balance in manufactured goods has deteriorated so sharply tells exactly this tale. Where precisely has the damage been done? Cars lead the Hall of Shame, although the commercial vehicle business, once the pride

177

and joy of the North, isn't far behind. Both weigh in over the half-billion mark, that being the fearsome extent to which the 1983 trade balance for each fell short of 1982.

Alas, the litany of woe stoppeth not. An excellent article in the *Financial Times* also bewailed the decline of chemicals, construction equipment, textiles, aero engines and gas turbines, and piston engines. Nor was it just the sunset industries that were sinking – sunrise scientific apparatus, photographic equipment, and electronic components also figured in the falls, followed by the more down-to-earth (*sic*) farm equipment, pumps, and compressors. So what else is left?

If the slide goes much further, the only sectors sure of their export surpluses will be those in which foreigners can't compete – like genuine Scotch whisky. Whatever part the level of the pound does or doesn't play in these reverses, something else plainly matters far more: sheer lack of competitive power, based on world-ranking products and processes. Failures of marketing, at home and overseas, doubtless do their bit, too: but the words of *FT* writer Ian Rodger have the ring of ominous truth: 'It is hard to see what the substitute might be for the big, high-value end-products of engineering. . . . Somehow, Britain has to rebuild some world leaders in these areas.'

That is infinitely easier said than done. The manufacturing base in vehicles, to take the prime offender, has been so sawn away that a comeback to world leadership is out of any question. In many sectors, far-sighted companies have been shrinking UK operations to their viable cores and/or building up other assets overseas – notably in America. To move away from engineering, that's what Beecham did to raise US turnover to 28 per cent of its total, closing fast on the share coming from a British market where the company's main brands were distinctly mature, while also offsetting some of the sluggishness from another ripe line, antibiotics.

Its US buys in toiletries, pharmacy products, home care, and perfumery are several and solid. But early in 1984 *Business Week* pointed out one mighty snag (along with the predictable lesser ones of marketing and takeover problems in the seething US market): Beecham 'is butting up against consumer product companies that dwarf it in revenues and resources', and which can bring backbreaking and possibly overweening market pressure to bear. Beecham will have its own ideas about that. But if the general point is true (and it is) of a company as vast, vigorous, and victorious as this (with £1.7

billion of 1982–3 sales), the world prognosis for smaller and/or less sturdy UK firms looks dismal whichever way they turn.

The Nuggets in Niches

That last point applies even to the exploding new high technology and information technology markets. Few analogies have caught on faster than that between the dawn of the automobile and the age of the personal computer. The similarity that has received most excited attention, though, is not just the proliferation of makes, but the possibility of computers emulating American (and British) cars in massive brand extinction. Are the failures of Osborne, Dragon and Tycom, for example, the precursor of the collapses that left GM, Ford, Chrysler (and Lord Nuffield) in command?

It can be argued that, unlike the car of the twenties, the computer of the eighties is strictly an assembly job. Far from making its own engines, gearboxes, and axles, even IBM, as noted, buys in the entire kit and caboodle for its Personal Computer. Thus the economies of scale don't work in favour of the integrated producer – there being no such thing. The argument contains an incontrovertible truth that applies to many markets. Ease of production, often for reasons akin to those in home computers, has resulted in ease of entry; and costs of production, being roughly equal, in many cases no longer rule the roost. What does? Technical strengths (like logic arrays and software) may still give a mighty advantage to the big battalions. But so, above all, will marketing. Given the vastly greater spending power of the IBMs and Apples, let alone the Hewlett-Packards, Wangs, and DECs, and given that the latter, despite their technological power and financial muscle, have been having such trouble in the home computer market, the chances can't really be good for weaker firms with minority sales.

There will, of course, be a rich market for those serving genuine minorities with special products that suit particular purposes. In the computer market the profitable survivors will include both those who reap the economies of marketing scale and those niche sellers who play BMW to the great man's Volkswagen – and sometimes (like BMW) steal the show. Any marketing company must make this strategic choice between specialization and generalization, and it's no use choosing the latter without the necessary general strength.

The truth is doubly and trebly confirmed by an interesting study from McKinsey consultants Richard E. Cavanagh and Donald K. Clifford. It shows that America's profitable 'mid-sized' companies wisely shun mass markets in favour of niches. But middling is as middling does: the definition of mid-sized is sales ranging from $25 million to a billion – and that was the *1971* figure in 1982 dollars. Nor are the fast-growing US middleweights exclusively technological; the likes of Dunkin' Donuts stress that low-tech can create a rich niche just as readily as high.

To cook up niche success, however, not only must you first catch your niche; you must fatten it up for the long-term pot. Here lies the significance of the fact that, with the highly special exception of BL, none of the London Stock Exchange's super-winners of 1983 (whether capitalized over or under £50 million) manufactured consumer goods fit to set the welkin ringing. The same, to be fair, is true of the super-losers; although the latter do include, sadly, several companies whose strategies seemed the model for success.

The missing mass-marketers nearly all owe their absence to having had to face restricted sales growth, huge promotion and distribution costs, and permanently squeezed margins; in contrast, share losers like Racal (shares down 32 per cent) and UEI (down 51 per cent) were positioned in growth sectors, where precise targeting on defined market niches is supposed to yield consistent and rapid sales rises, with lofty margins won from proprietary technology. The theory is fine: but, as always in management, practice has the last word.

The first rumble of trouble at Racal – a marked drop in 1982–3 profitability – rubbed in the blindingly obvious truth that hi-tech is also high-risk: a truism much ignored on both sides of the Atlantic in the quest of electronic gold. Characteristically, the hi-tech niche yields its ripest rewards when the exploitation is least mature – hence the up-rush of BSR's share price (283 per cent in 1983) on the initial results of rejuvenation by computer devices made in Hong Kong. If that trebling seems startling, consider the fortunes of one US company, TeleVideo Systems, whose happy ex-Korean proprietor, K. Philip Hwang, has become half a billionaire.

Hwang makes more VDUs, apparently, than anybody in the world save IBM. That's a vital clue. Within the profitable niche, the modern marketer must achieve international spread and clear leadership to be reasonably sure of success everlasting. Far better to be Japan's Epson,

180

with half the market in printers for computers, than just slugging it out with the champs in personal computers or getting stuck in too narrow a niche.

The Double D Approach

The logic of those segmented, niche markets explains why one management doctrine above all is spreading so swiftly, even among the beached whales of the business world. The notion is that large companies should be divided into profit centres built round clearly defined markets, and placed under the equally clear leadership of managers who are instructed to get onwards and upwards, or out.

It's the antithesis of the once equally fashionable idea of packing some skyscraper with Superminds who would co-ordinate, compel and control everything – but couldn't. The new trend doesn't only reflect such past failures, which are legion. More important, it's a response to the fragmentation of markets into segments, often dominated by unique technologies, techniques, and trading patterns. That now gives the old Double D (Decentralize and Delegate) a far better chance. At the corporate centre, he who doesn't delegate is lost in the complexities of markets he can't hope to manage from afar.

The extent to which this logic has been taken by the best-managed companies is remarkable. IBM not only set up an independent group for the afore-mentioned PC, but, as noted, allowed it to place the crucial work (chips, software, and all) outside IBM – an action which would once have been rank heresy. In Japan, Canon based a corporate turnround in part on a division by products, which gave the new groups their own reorganized factories and R&D facilities. Again, the results were spectacular.

It's a mistake, though, to attribute those results solely or even principally to the Double D. Decentralization and delegation should be slaves to the master plan of the corporate centre – whose role is made more, not less, important by the development of niche markets. The Achilles heel of the new segmentation could be failure at the centre of companies to grasp that the vital central role includes imposing the common culture that makes an IBM even stronger than its parts and strengthens the parts in turn. The market niche has become a necessity: but it offers no hiding place from the other corporate essentials.

Heller's Golden Rules

HOW TO . . .

. . . MANAGE DIVERSITY
1: Don't buy markets or market share – buy profits
2: Don't try to manage diversity unless you know how to
3: Give multi-form businesses the same concentration as unitary ones

. . . USE AQUISITION
1: Only diversify to add strength to the basic business
2: Allow separate businesses to keep separate market identities
3: When buying a business, make sure the planning, cost and execution are all equally right

. . . COPE WITH DISCONTINUITY
1: Make the customer king: know your competitor: know the company man next door: move fast: and supersede your own miracle before somebody else does
2: In the newest markets and businesses, stick to the oldest marketing rules
3: To win long–term market share, invest, innovate and create value

. . . MANAGE CHANGE
1: If you can't beat 'em, join 'em in any way that makes sense
2: Organize the company round its markets, not the other way round
3: Remember that 'the main job of distribution . . . is to tell production what it ought to make'

. . . POSITION THE BUSINESS
1: Move up the market and towards the consumer
2: Aim for niches where you can build long-term success
3: Follow the Double D doctrine – Decentralize and Delegate

SECTION SIX
GROWTH

1: All Good Things. . .

Marketers must have vision: the formation of dreams is romantic and thrilling, and their realization is the foundation of futures – Honda's first successful bike wasn't called the Dream for nothing. But the real point is realism itself. Managers whose future dreams are unrealistic run the risk of pursuing equally unrealistic policies in the present – and that way disaster lies.

Sometimes the failure is more one of words than one of deeds – for example, when a senior executive once urged would-be wage strikers not to impede BL's progress towards becoming (like tomorrow) 'the best car company there has ever been'. Even allowing for the fact that the executive concerned was supremo of the salesmen, a breed not known for aversion to hyperbole, that was going too far at a time when it would have been an economic miracle if BL actually broke even on schedule. If break-even is 'best', how would making a profit rank?

The words are individual, but the point is general. Realism is the foundation on which enthusiasm can work managerial and marketing miracles: hard, cruel, merciless realism. Once retire behind clouds of self-deception, and the company is desperately vulnerable. Why did bid victim Berec's directors persist year after year with research spending that was only 1 per cent of turnover? Was it because they thought this a realistic level of spending that would keep them ahead in marketplaces as technological as batteries? Or did they keep on reassuring themselves that theirs was the best of all companies with the best of all possible products?

Time and again, some such thesis as the latter is swallowed hook, line, and sinker – making a vice out of necessity. The necessity is often that the company can't actually afford the necessary spending. Caught between necessities, the management allows its marketing strength to ooze away as under-investment saps the ability to compete. That's why those attending while some major section of UK industry is letting down its hair hear a constant refrain – Britain is slow. Slow to take up new end-use possibilities. Slow to adopt new processes. Slow to use new materials.

The slowness reflects deep uncertainty about demand, returns on investment, availability of funds, etc. But that doesn't excuse avoidance of the competitive facts, or ignoring the inevitable consequences of lagging behind for the future of the business. These slow horses put on their own blinkers. And the blinkers are made of delusions like (in the extreme cases) becoming 'the best car company there has ever been'. Realism is the only safeguard.

The Market Always Wins

Let realism out of the door, and grandiose delusions fly in the window. Firms begin to act under the fatal misapprehension that they, not their customers, make the market – and in that process they may ignore the best of business advice: 'Be greedy, but not too greedy.' The travails of the warring auction tribes, Sotheby's and Christie's, almost certainly began when they imposed the so-called 'buyer's premium' of 10 per cent on top of the traditional 'seller's premium' of the same amount.

Without calling on the services of a pocket calculator you can see that this handy stratagem doubles the auction house's gross take. Messrs S. and C. were grabbing £18.18 of every £100 contributed by the suckers – the buying public (Christie's has since cut its take). Worse still, the big suckers with the big collections and big pictures benefited from preferential rates, while the little suckers took it or left it. Increasingly they left it – or, rather, didn't take it in sufficient quantity **to finance the vast expansion on which both houses were bent.**

It's a tale as old as the woman who lived in a shoe. Companies riding a boom believe it will never end. That being so, any activity, however expensive, will prove to be self-financing as the good times roll. When (as happens to all men, or nearly all) the bad times roll instead, the ex-boomers find themselves like the Old Woman again – they have so many children that they don't know what to do. Sooner or later, though, they find the answer – Sotheby's had to fire 200 out of 1,000 employees in New York for starters.

At that, the Manhattan operation was positively skeleton-staffed compared to London. A service business like auctioneering depends on low costs, excellent service, acceptable prices, acute sensitivity to the customer (who is all they've got), and avoidance of extravagant capital commitments. In their ferocious battle with each other, the twain Tweedledeed and Tweedeldummed themselves into a situation for which, ultimately, nobody else is to blame.

The degree to which the market is or isn't satisfied always calls the tune. If ever a business appears to be successfully ignoring the logic of markets, don't believe it – because, nine times out of ten, if not 99 times out of 100, logic will win. The falling apart of IBH, the construction equipment colossus stitched together by Horst-Dieter Esch, was just such a severe blow to those who hope that circles can be squared. The Esch theory was that, by sewing together firms that have separately failed in weak markets, you end up with a group that is strong – strong enough to compete with the likes of Caterpillar, once one of the most admired marketers on (or in) earth.

But in an era when Caterpillar was crawling through heavy losses, how could an accumulation of feebler competitors hope to survive? True, Esch mostly got his companies for next to nothing from owners (ranging from General Motors to Powell Duffryn) who were only too glad to offload these burdens. But the process gives a new twist to Lord Duveen's famous advice to art-buying millionaires – 'If you're buying the priceless, you're getting it cheap.' In commerce, the valueless is probably dear – it would have taken miracles to make a silk purse out of Esch's collection of sow's ears.

In fairness, some of his companies were much better than others. But in the aftermath of the IBH receivership, the truth emerged that in several vital respects IBH had done too little to make marketing or manufacturing sense of its acquisitions. For instance, similar IBH products with different brands were still being sold through the same outlets. While Esch had shown a pan-European vision that was admirable, and financial dexterity that was prodigious to the point of utter recklessness, in the basic business of making and selling his weaknesses would have worked against IBH in better markets.

But in a world where construction equipment demand was down by 30–50 per cent, IBH hadn't an earthly. Not that Caterpillar's fate has been shared by everybody – its Japanese competitor, Komatsu, has stayed in profit, taking advantage of the recession to make huge inroads into the US firm's market share, which as recently as 1981 came to around 50 per cent, against 15 per cent for Komatsu. The latter's sales were only 38 per cent behind Caterpillar by 1983; further tribute to Japan Inc., you might think.

But you'd be wrong. The non-existent Inc. (in the shape of MITI) actually let Caterpillar into Japan via a joint company with the ultra-powerful Mitsubishi. Confidently expected to crumble, Komatsu did nothing of the sort. Instead, it set its sights squarely on the giant, making 'Maru-C' (or encircle Caterpillar) its motto, and fighting ferociously to undercut Caterpillar on price (by 10–15 per cent) while excelling it on service – and also challenging very strongly on technology.

The Japanese were also quicker to anticipate the Middle East construction surge, whose reversal explains so much of the subsequent world market collapse. In comparison to Komatsu's concentrated, centralized, comprehensive drive, the over-expanding Esch empire had little to offer. But, then, who can compete with a Japanese company whose boss once said, 'You can't get by just doing your best'?

When Good's No Good

That is the vital, unforgettable moral. No matter how good you think you are, no matter how strongly your business is booming, you are not good enough. If you believe that you are, sooner or later the figures will prove you wrong. The answer to the question – when is a great marketing company not a great company? – is clear: when it doesn't produce great results.

Thus the market leader in many booming British trades is Boots, the master in several segments which have starred in the Great Recession. That recession, anyway, has spared the High Streets to some considerable extent: but it hasn't spared Boots. The slightly mind-boggling fact is that this most homely of all household names increased turnover by roughly two-thirds from 1978–9 to 1982–3, but its net profit of £78 million was up by only 5.7 per cent on that of four years back.

Before tax and interest, Boots' margins on turnover, 15.6 per cent at the start of the decade, were precisely half that level in 1983. To put it another way round: over the whole ten years, while turnover quadrupled, profits only doubled, with three-quarters of the increase taking place before 1977–8. What was going on?

It couldn't, presumably, have been the build-up of the own-brands which have, on the whole, only enhanced Boots' fine reputation. It couldn't have been the determined diversification into hardware, like the current push into personal computers. It couldn't have been general pressure on margins in chemists' goods – whatever the pressure, it can hardly have been as severe as that on supermarkets; and Tesco, a company whose fallen idol status (in contrast to that of Boots) is well known, did little worse than the latter in the same period.

Neither should the other leg of Boots (so to speak) have been at fault: the fact that it also manufactured pharmaceuticals. That's the very market where Glaxo found glory – doubling after-tax profits in four years even before the full impact of its Zantac drug (which threatens to give SmithKline, makers of the rival Tagamet, the very ulcers these products are designed to relieve). As noted in Section 5, Chapter 4, Glaxo, probably cleverly, has teamed up with Swiss Hoffmann-La Roche to tackle Tagamet more effectively in the main arena, the US, where Boots also had high hopes, which rested on giving its Brufen anti-inflammatory drug the Big Push.

Obviously, an American drug victory would transform the Boots picture. But it wouldn't answer the invidious question of why the picture needed transformation – and major transformation at that. It's tempting to draw an analogy between the Boots of the past few years and the Marks & Spencer of the 1960s – another visibly great business that was then visibly not sustaining its growth image, despite expansion of both square footage and foods.

M&S broke out of that impasse by breaking with some of its own past traditions – becoming more fashion- and variety-conscious for a start. It's somewhat pointless to have the right stores, the right goods, and the right image in the right markets if you don't get the right results – and you won't get those unless the vision of the future is accompanied by and built on a clear, realistic vision of the present. In the case of Boots, that real view would have shown, among other things, that its sales per employee were far too low compared with those of its more profitable competitors. And it is from such unpleasant realities that the most rewarding visions of the future can be most easily constructed – and most readily realized.

2: Failure Has Too Few Friends

In any market, any company is liable to make mistakes. Some will be part of the normal learning process, and their correction will in turn form part of the company's marketing strength. But the 'out of weakness came forth strength' routine is even more important when the error is abnormal and gross. The greatest error, in fact, is to perpetuate an offence: especially if the main reason is that managers gang up round the *status quo*.

The example of Waterford Glass is one not to be ignored. Few companies in the British Isles, let alone in Eire, could have matched the performance of a company whose figures showed an unbroken series of rises, which took it from £1.3 million of profits in 1970 to £11.6 million in 1979. The series was broken in 1981, when, on a 13.7 per cent rise in turnover, the company's pre-tax profits fell by 31 per cent. However, Noel Griffin, the managing director, reacted with the following comment: 'It's about time. The group needed a shock to get itself back into line.'

Griffin could quite easily have rested on some statement like those of the British giants weighing in at the same time with far more dreadful figures. 'All the economic factors have been very adverse,' as one of the bleeding mammoths said. But it's not what hits you, nor even why, that counts: it's what you propose to do about it. Waterford should have been shock-proof, occupying a marketing stance as near to perfect as this imperfect world can offer. World demand for its cut-crystal wares wasn't flagging even while the economic climate worsened: 'unabated' is Griffin's word for his market. Year after year the product has been on allocation, the prices have been wonderfully elastic (in the upwards direction), the competition virtually non-existent. So what went wrong?

The main point is that managers in Waterford's wonderful position have to maintain a delicate balancing act: keeping the market under-supplied, but not by too much. The balance was disturbed in the first half of the bad year by a drop in productivity: 'absenteeism', says Griffin, was the problem. Whether the cause is delinquent workers or deficient management, the moral is the same. Effective, reliable production is the foundation of marketing success – a truth which Waterford has turned to great advantage down the years.

But it's also no surprise to learn that Waterford, like so many other firms, had diversified into other activities to reduce its potential over-dependence on one product. All that usually happens, of course, is that, far from acting as an extra float, one or more of the diversified interests becomes a dead weight. In Waterford's case, the 1980 villain was retailing, where profits all but disappeared. None too bright diversifications are among the errors with which groups tend to live too easily, while otherwise enjoying twenty-five years of continuous and immensely profitable growth. That's why a little misfortune may, as Griffin suggested, be an almost necessary blow – provided that the shocked management really does get itself back into line.

Big Base Complacency

In some cases, however great the shock, either nothing happens at all; or too little happens; or a lot happens, but too late. The results are painfully visible in the affairs of Fisons in fertilizers, GKN in nuts and bolts, and Dunlop in tyres: all British giants forced to abandon production, not just in a base business, but one on which all or much of their history, reputation, and fame were founded.

To get some idea of the enormity, merely think the impossible thought of IBM copping out of computers, Daimler-Benz deserting cars, or Sony audio recorders. To be fair, tyres, fertilizers, and fasteners are markets which, through no fault of any individual firm, have soured. Not that the individuals were faultless, though: to be over-manned, over-borrowed, and under-competitive in a strong market is a sorry burden: in a weak market, it's an inescapable catastrophe.

Dunlop's besetting domestic weakness, visible as long ago as 1969, was its over-dependence on original equipment sales to UK car firms: not a particularly good idea even at the time. In the untied replacement market Dunlop's lack of all-round marketing wizardry showed up in a notably lower share. Far more serious, however, the group's very early European and world expansion didn't feed back into greater domestic strength. On the contrary, the horny hand of Fort Dunlop, Birmingham, lay heavy on the Continental interests, and Dunlop first lagged fatefully behind the radial revolution launched by European rivals, then, after belated conversion, opted wrongly for textile cord instead of steel.

All that, however, is in the gory past (bloody to the tune of £120 million of group losses in four years). What lessons does hindsight teach? Or, rather, what would due foresight have predicated? First, the basic objective of a market leader must be prowess in productivity, with the lowest costs in the least factories. That championship goes hand in hand, obviously enough, with (second) cornering the most wondrous production technology which money can buy. That in turn links intimately with (third) the absolute and burning need for the brightest and best product technology. Fourth, all of the above must be cemented by unbeatably strong branding, of the corporation and its product lines; Michelin has been far more effective in this department, as in its radial technology. Fifth, you need the rare big business courage, when all around are generously expanding capacity, to restrict yours parsimoniously to what can realistically be utilized at a truly ripe return.

Finally, the company must be marketing-led to the last detail. Even in sporting goods, for one small example, ads for Dunlop's running shoe seem to have appeared far more than the shoes themselves; Adidas, Nike, New Balance *et al* monopolized the shelf space. Generally, in Dunlop's non-tyre rump businesses (£635 million of 1982 sales), there was urgent need for transformation, judged by their measly £20 million of operating profits. Those big base businesses, alas, easily breed complacency, and that's a hard habit to break, save in desperate adversity: by then, the pledge may be taken too late to save the ravaged vitals.

Where Real Safety Lies

The all-too-obvious moral has become blatant, impossible to ignore with any degree of safety, now that the times are a-changing at such monstrous pace. Merely consider the extraordinary plight of Sony.

191

From its first invasion of the tape recorder market, Sony has shown a sureness of foot compounded equally of technological brilliance and marketing skills – especially needed because it started so far behind other Japanese electrical giants in the furiously competitive home market.

Yet in 1982–3 Sony's profits sunk, weighed down, above all, by a collapse in world market share in VCRs. Back in 1976 Sony had two-thirds of this market. In 1983 it was clinging on for dear life to 12 per cent, about a quarter of the share won by Matsushita (taking in the half-owned JVC) with the rival and now triumphant VHS system. Despite its strengths in audio, despite its dazzling coup with the Walkmans and the Watchmans, despite its dominance in some professional markets, Sony suddenly looked strangely vulnerable; particularly since its filmless camera seems to have been exposed too early.

The problem of excessive dependence on consumer markets has been compounded by the defeat in VCRs – possibly the last great boom market in home entertainment for many years. If the Matsushita and Sony roles were reversed, Sony would have had less urgent need for the office products (of the present, never mind the future) in which it had so weak a position – computers, facsimile machines, copiers, typewriters, etc. But without strengths in these markets, how will Sony keep its position in the technological race?

Nobody contemplating Sony's future in this alarmingly competitive context should feel any *Schadenfreude*. There but for the grace of God goes anybody. Even in large new markets like VCRs, one false step into technology or marketing can mean a permanently broken leg. Even the winner, JVC, could be ruptured by forces beyond its control. Its profits were forced down by voluntary restraints on VCR exports to Europe, at a time, though, when Hitachi reported itself 15 per cent up – with its VCR sales especially massive. In the current phase of cut-throat competition, the good giants seem to be getting greater: and the mere middle-sized have a dangerously increasing amount to prove.

Indeed, there is no safety anywhere – not even with products that sit on top of the world for quality, luxury and reputation. Take Wedgwood, Rolls-Royce Motors, and the previously mentioned Waterford Glass. All three, very obviously, depend on the American market for their health and strength. When the legions of rich US consumers are off their feed, no marketing power on earth can protect a luxury china, glass, or car business from feeling undernourished.

But what happened? In 1983, to recover US sales, Rolls-Royce, as noted earlier, had to cut its prices – an unheard-of act of self-inflicted *lèse-majesté*. Waterford's long years of uninterrupted profit growth had come to an abrupt end in 1979. Wedgwood also went ex-growth with a bang; it produced profit figures that would have seemed off-colour in 1973–4, when total sales were a mere quarter of the level ten years on.

The breakdown of Wedgwood's sales had, of course, changed markedly over the period. The people who run top-of-the-market companies are not blind to the obvious: over-exposure to America is only the most glaring aspect of a market situation in which, by definition, saturation can never be far away. After all, nobody needs these costly goodies; purchase is indefinitely postponable; and it only takes a relatively small number of postponements for growth to cease entirely. *Ergo* the prudent company diversifies, going down-market in its main business, or striking out geographically, or adding entirely new markets – as Waterford did with things like greetings cards and fine china, but, as noted, with no very brilliant results.

As for Rolls-Royce, it sought shelter in the hugely diversified embrace of Vickers, thus utterly and evidently changing the nature and scope of top management's problems, but making them no easier. The same is true of the other luxuriators. Running a business concentrated round one basic, strong, and clearly identifiable theme is a different game entirely from trying to make financial sense out of a clutch of companies or countries.

The strategy adopted by Moët Hennessy looks much more promising: stringing together the leading champagne house by far with a top name in brandy and with other upper-crust *marques* like Dior perfumes. Recession in luxury markets will still hit the whole company, but probably in uneven fashion – and at least the management problems will be in the same language. By Sod's Law, it is almost certain that interests bought to counterbalance the existing base business will reserve their own nastiest surprises for the moment when they are least welcome: when the long-loved luxury is also down on its luck. The real safety lies only in learning the lessons of failure and repeating those of success. A management with its eyes open will find plenty of both in its own experiences.

3: Investing Is Success

In today's naked markets, investing is success. If a company can't afford to finance investment in new products, processes, and markets, it is already failing – and it will fail still more in the future (if it has one). If there's a single lesson which Western business needs to learn from the Japanese, this is it. But even those Westerners who have seized hold of the lesson have sometimes grasped it only dimly.

Consider this observation: 'We have a five-year perspective to break even. It's what I'd call a Japanese approach.' Thus spoke the Frankfurt marketing director of the *Financial Times*, adding a new phrase to the Marketing Man's lexicon of useful euphemisms. All over the West companies in similar positions, losing money on projects that were either misconceived or mistimed, have consoled themselves with the thought that they were really dynamic thrusters *à la Japonaise*, breaking into new markets on a long-term strategy.

Even the Japanese reality doesn't bear out this engaging myth. The most celebrated breakthrough is probably Toyota's penetration of the US market. It took seventeen years before Toyota toppled VW off its peak as leading importer. The first Crowns blew up on the Californian freeways – only the grisly start of a long saga of blood, sweat, and tears: what the Japanese saw as a potential Pearl Harbor became the equivalent of Mao's Long March. Nobody goes voluntarily into that kind of torture. Given its time over again, Toyota would have done very differently – and so, I doubt not, would the *FT*.

How much the *FT* has truly suffered in following its 'five-year perspective' is known only to the keepers of its books. But its managing director once observed that 'It costs us around £2 million a year to print in Frankfurt rather than distribute from here.' Assuming that all its 33,000 overseas sales came from Germany, that added up to over £2 a week per extra subscriber to the paper (sales abroad had doubled since Frankfurt began). And who is to say how many of these extra sales could have been obtained from London printing? Or how much of the extra £16 million of (presumably) European advertising revenue the *FT* really, in its spokesman's words, 'wouldn't have gained if we hadn't been there'?

That is apparently the equation on which the *FT* was relying to pass break-even at its 'branch factory' in Frankfurt. The boss compared its extra costs with the colossal expense of flying 7,000 copies a day to Scotland. But, of course, this analogy broke down at once. The *FT* couldn't have maintained its basic marketing stance as the all-British, all-leading financial paper if it had started leaving out inconvenient bits of the UK.

Frankfurt was (in truth) a greenfields project, a new venture in its own right, in which the management was not, like its lately discovered Japanese models, breaking new export ground for established products; the *FT* has striven to create a new market for English-language, trans-European business papers. In those pioneering circumstances, it's lucky, to quote the Frankfurt man again, that the pioneers' 'view has not been to make money very quickly'. They won't.

It's no secret that the *FT* was inspired less by the example of Japan than by the fear of the *Wall Street Journal* possibly coming to Europe. Possibility became actuality – and it certainly took Japanese, if not Dutch, courage for the *Journal* to launch in Europe in the middle of a world recession, and at a time when the wind bore grisly rumours of collapses among the very banks on whom it had to depend for much of its advertising. But that was only one of the myriad acts of commercial bravery which first made it clear that, while the smoke of deep recession still obscured the battlefield, the Western economy was on the march.

Even in Britain, the longest battered by slump, when industrial production was slithering around at a level just below that of a decade back, the micro-managers of Britain, within that miserable macrocosm, were proliferating new marketing plans and products. It doesn't matter that, in the nature of things, such plans will sometimes be half-baked or will misfire; or that 'new' will often be a euphemism

195

for rehashed or me-too. The urge is what counts – the impetus that made an Elida Gibbs (at last) splurge £825,000 on persuading a recumbent Astral skin cream to pick up its bed and walk; the urge that led an Associated Newspapers to send still more good money, via a colour supplement, where £15 million had already gone to launch *Mail on Sunday*; that kind of courage is essential to the marketer's kit.

The Lessons of Lazell

Nor is courage confined to fast-moving consumer goods and media. The last few years have seen report after report of brave new ventures in such things as pay-TV, computer graphics, identification systems, scientific graphics computing, etc. The nature of these projects, of course, sticks out several miles: they are all in the waters of the higher technology, which are spreading to engulf all of traditional engineering – and which offer in the process those segmented opportunities for which the bravest and best marketers have been searching.

But new technology doesn't mean new principles – nor even new industries. The guiding principle is challenge: investment in technology, like investment in marketing, is the power-house for challenging the established position of others, or for challenging the market itself, by creating new dimensions. On this criterion, at one post-war point, in what later won that ugly name of fast-moving consumer goods, there was only one real contender for the title, 'best manager in Britain': H.G. Lazell, architect of the Beecham Group, who died in 1982 at the age of seventy-nine. He was the exponent of a style of management which, if it had only attracted more imitators, would have rewritten much of Britain's deeply disappointing performance after 1968 (the year when Lazell retired).

Here are some of the great man's major themes. First, if you want to beat 'em, fight 'em. Seeing correctly that American companies would try to set the pace in post-war Europe, Lazell decided that Beecham could never compete here unless it could challenge and succeed there – in the US, as it did with Brylcreem and Macleans. Second, Macleans had become the cornerstone of Beecham's growth after Lazell, who became an accountant the hard way, supported Sir Alexander Maclean, with pen and paper, by showing that the latter won even more gigantic profits by selling his own brand than by supplying chemists with private label toothpaste. Lazell thus established two principles: that, in modern marketing, the pen is mightier than the hunch, and that branding is the true name of the game.

Third, Lazell hated his challenges to fail, but never let failure deter him. The disaster of Silvikrin shampoo in the US (the name killed it dead among a nation of macho males who dreaded grey hair) was taken in a broken stride – and a later generation of managers triumphed there again with Aquafresh toothpaste. Fourth, such triumphs were founded on the fact that Lazell, a professional manager himself, staffed his group with trained people who followed the same canon – whether in the toiletries, food, or pharmaceuticals businesses that he developed so powerfully.

Fifth, in the latter activity, Lazell never allowed his belief that investment in research was the key to success to be shaken by decades of no reward. He was finally vindicated by the synthetic penicillins that have underpinned much of Beecham's post-Lazell growth. But that was only after mastering a sixth principle: that concentration is the key to success in R&D, as in most of management. The lesson applies to advertising, too. Lazell used to say that he didn't mind what the advertisements said about Macleans, so long as they said it made teeth whiter. More foolish marketing men have forgotten that advertising is in part (in major part) about repetition, just as they have forgotten (or never knew) that investment is doubly the key to marketing success.

Money Is the Root of All Virtue

This ignorance, however, became much less blissful and much less general in the Big Squeeze of the early eighties. Adversity is an excellent teacher. In the food industry, for instance, with one arm of the Iron Maiden of recession throttling revenues, and the other pressing on costs, the nature of the struggle was clear. Only higher productivity could open the door to higher margins; manufacturers duly became intent on cutting labour costs. One survey showed 85 per cent of food manufacturers intending to spend the same or more money on plant and machinery; mostly to boost productivity, for which, alas, read unemployment – almost two-thirds expected their investment spending to cut numbers employed. Sad – but in food, as in other industries, Britain is no longer the low-cost producer: witness the serried imports in every grocery store. Investment in de-manning has become an essential ingredient of the productivity mix – and thus of the marketing one.

But investment means goodies as well. In the same survey, a nourishing 82 per cent of the food companies planned to invest more than replacement needs – and over half included new product work in their plans. The opportunity to cash in on product differentiation has scaled new peaks in recent years, which have seen consumers switching towards the nutritious, unfattening, stodgeless, and exotic. Not only do these lissom qualities offer the hope of higher prices; they are one way to break the hammerlock which, given half a chance, the retailers have applied and will go on applying.

The supermarkets can exert their own version of the Big Squeeze even on some supplier who has 65 per cent of the market – double the national share of even the biggest retailer. In fact, a manufacturer's 65 per cent may be only a tiny fraction of a supermarket's total trade, so advantage over the retailer can be gained much less easily by muscle (of which the latter has plenty), than by innovative, irresistible consumer appeal, which is aimed at raising margins and return on investment. In marketing, money is the root of all virtue – and without putting enough of it into innovative investment, a manufacturer will be in the Big Squeeze for ever. In fact, 2.7 per cent of the above sample thought they would be, anyway: they were wrong. The future is bright with naked, unsqueezed opportunity – but only for those who are prepared to create, grasp, and finance the opportune investment.

4: The Inertial Drip-Feed

Failure may have few friends, but it has plenty of remedies: so many and so well-known that nobody attempting a turnround from disaster lacks for examples and precepts. But how do you tackle what is usually a far more difficult problem? How do you cope with success?

The problem is two-fold. Not only does a smash marketing hit, like a personal triumph, often go to the head: but the winning company, bumptious or not, will sooner or later face real and agonizing questions of how to build on and sustain its success. A writer in the *Harvard Business Review*, Thomas V. Bonoma, came up with a telling phrase to describe one aspect of this potential crisis; 'marketing inertia' – the title of an article which takes a swipe at some famous US names for getting stuck with ideas of their own marketing brilliance, even though the ideas were founded on enormous market success.

Thus Texas Instruments passionately believes that 'low prices lead to market share dominance'. Sounds O.K. – but wait. TI followed this philosophy when marketing its cheaper calculators at discount prices through the department stores and other mass outlets. It thus neatly pole-axed its standing with the office equipment specialists, who had been selling Texas Instruments' more expensive, higher-margin machines. In 1981, after similar pursuit of the cheap and dominant, TI had to withdraw in disarray from the watch market. A couple of years later, exactly the same fate overtook its home computers. Low-priced, mass-volume consumption goods just aren't its bag.

Then there is Coors, the American beer which became famous for the quality ('product superiority') to which the family management attributed their success. Bonoma points out that 'quality is determined more by customers' preferences than by family formulas' – and, in the case of Coors, customers preferred a beer that they could actually buy. Poor distribution made the quality quite academic. At Coors, as at TI, marketing actions were attuned, not to the market, but to preconceived notions of how it would or should behave.

How do you cure inertia? The first stage is to find out if you've got it. You may get the answer to 'Are we inert?' from market share and profitability trends, but you're far more likely to find out the awful truth away from the office: Bonoma thus mentions managers who spend one day a month on a tour of both important and average accounts. He also suggests restructuring the market-men: preferably organizing them round major market groups, rather than round the products the company just happens to make. Then, there's praise for AT&T's recruitment of an executive whose job description was 'manager in charge of shaking things up'.

But what if the company is held to be wholly successful, not only by its own management, but by everybody outside? If the company obviously needs shaking up, it's easy: the standard device is to introduce marked change at the top – by importing a manager from another industry (as Atari did by picking a Philip Morris man whose background in cigarettes could hardly have been further from computers and video games). Another favoured technique, in a family-dominated company, is to appoint a chief executive who is not a family member.

In crisis that device has often worked well – as when, long ago, young Henry Ford II turned in great travail to Ernest R. Breech. But when the chief executive torch at the successful Marks & Spencer passed to a non-familial manager, the case for fundamental change was far less clear-cut. Nor was the new leader, Sir Derek Rayner, a newly made broom. After his long years in the country's most admired retail chain, Sir Derek was as thoroughly indoctrinated in the group's culture as any one in the Sieff family. That corporate culture, in turn, must be among the most powerful ever created: as you'd only expect when so many forceful men have concentrated on so narrow a front for so long.

But maybe that raised the crucial question. Was the front, for all the product diversification of recent years, including the food expansion fathered by Rayner's predecessor, Lord Sieff, still too narrow? A business whose shops are obviously so good, by subjective and objective standards, is desperately hard to criticize. But if you adjust the group's rise in earnings per share for inflation (as *Management Today* does annually), the result was negative over the decade to 1982: a 2.4 per cent annual *decline.*

True, that was better than 127 other companies in Britain's top 200. But that still can't dispel the nagging feeling that so intensively managed and superbly integrated an operation should have generated greater rewards. The reasons why it hasn't are obvious. Britain's sluggish economy has inevitably cramped the style of a group which was largely confined to those stagnant shores, which has near-saturation shares of mature markets, and within which that all-powerful culture was dead set on organic growth, not acquisition. When these characteristics were described to an American financier wanting to know if Marks might like to take a billion-dollar retail bauble off his hands, he listened in silence, then said: 'I seem to have picked on exactly the wrong company.' He sure had.

Maybe the missing phase in the great chain's development would have made it the *right* company. After all, Sears Roebuck in the United States would be a mere smidgen of its $27.4 billion size (eight and a half times that of M&S) had it stuck to mail order. The evidence is that Marks has long been pressing against the natural and national barriers to the expansion of its magnificent patented method: the vertically integrated, limited catalogue variety store, stocking own-brand merchandise and steadily expanding the lines and sidelines. The way out is either to export the method (begun, but Marks has found the overseas sledding slow and sometimes painful), or to follow Sears in adding other consumer-based operations.

In the great Marks and Sieff eras, the company did not bring its usual scrupulous intensity to exploiting that base asset: its unique experience of the consumer. This could be because M&S has, in a sense, created its own consumers: the genius of its founders was to change people's buying habits and thus to turn a shop into a national brand. But serving mature markets in mature ways with a mature corporate culture is unlikely to produce rich growth.

The Electrifying Inertia

The great, sometimes stultifying, difficulty is that the imperatives of a new growth strategy and those of marketing inertia pull in opposite directions. Inertia shouldn't, surely, be powerful enough to win this tug-of-war. But its enormous pull can be judged by the way managements cling to businesses that, far from being successful, are chewing up pound notes. To prove the point, ask whether anybody in his right mind would retain a retailing business that lost 14 per cent on turnover year after year: surely not except for some incredibly compelling reason, or at the point of a gun?

Of course, in most cases the gun comes into play because of the losses: get into profit, or get out. Which is precisely the policy that the afore-mentioned company, actually the London Electricity Board, refused to apply to its retail establishments in 1982. Not that anybody could be sure that the High Street electricity showrooms had really lost nearly £7 million by their retailing brilliance in the previous four years. The figure is only an estimate. Anything more precise would be slightly difficult, judging by allegations that the LEB's accounting methods made it impossible to analyze the retailing losses accurately.

That figures, you might say. The single greatest cause of marketing failure is lack of accurate information. And the greatest cause of ignorance is seldom that the facts can't be found: rather, for whatever reason, people don't want to find them. Indeed, missing facts not only contribute to failures: they hide them. Suppose the books did show a 14 per cent negative return on the LEB's retail sales; it's hard to believe that the management could have brought itself to countenance that miserable reverse margin – what could possibly justify so large a loss? At the same time, when facts are simply absent (with leave), nobody need face up to their embarrassing implications, and the fail-unsafe situation is perpetuated.

Going deeper into the psychology of business inertia, managers tend to defend the marketing *status quo* with might and main, even though the one unchanging aspect of markets is that they change. All too often, suggest that a little market research wouldn't come amiss, and you're met with irrelevant appeals to long, arduous years of experience in the trade, with grumpy observations that the dubious assumptions being challenged are 'obvious': in short, with refusal to contemplate the painful process of thinking and acting anew.

Once, in the consumer durable dawn, the electricity supply industry may have had good reason to run its own shops. But today, with every High Street bristling with electrically powered goods, the retail side makes even less sense than the gas equivalent (which isn't saying much). And even if the £7 million loss estimate was out by half, that was still a grossly excessive cost to bear for a benefit which was, after all, invisible to the naked eye.

In the case of a publicly owned company like Texas Instruments, the pressures of investors and institutions are likely ultimately to reinforce reality and help to win the tug-of-war with inertia. The management must contend with two external groups, customers and shareholders, and however much it tries to ignore the first, the second will sooner or later catch on.

In the state-supported industries, management also has two main target groups – the same public, which (all too often) won't buy the goods and services in sufficient quantity and at high enough prices to cover costs: but, instead of shareholders, it has political overlords, who have to supply both any monetary difference and the ultimate monetary decisions. In a perfect world, success with group A would automatically bring success with B (as it does when A = customers and B = shareholders), but it ain't necessarily so. The more successful a state industry is (like the gas business in Britain), the more likely it is to suffer non-commercial pressure – for example, forcing it to surrender interests that no self-respecting private management would drop, or to exercise undue restraint on prices and profits.

The Putsch from Below

Curiously, though, the threatened assets which the gasmen were so anxious to retain included – yes, the High Street retail outlets. Yet could these pass marketing's basic test of profitability? Should they be retained if they can't? The highly favourable answers of middle managers actually involved in the showroom operations to the last question can probably be taken for granted. And there's the rub. Nor is it a dilemma that applies only in nationalized industries. The entire top management gets locked into the mentality of inertia, and it is rare indeed for the managerial peasants to revolt.

When they do, by the same token, the need for radical change must be overwhelming. In two cases, one semi-private, management uprisings at the beginning of the 1980s were in fact the prelude to massively needed change. One was the insubordination of rebellious managers at British Airways, sending a devastating critique of their bosses to Mrs Thatcher, smacking of a latter-day Peasants' Revolt.

203

The other was the way in which middle and senior managers at ICL bent any journalistic ear they could find with tales of their company's higher inadequacies. In both cases, and spectacularly soon, a top management topping followed. The push (or rather *putsch*) from below does, it seems, have its uses.

Or does it? On the one hand, the minds of top management would be wonderfully concentrated if they knew, say, that their performance was to be audited regularly by their underlings – with the audit results communicated to the public at large. But if the embattled bosses were to be asked for a similar account of their senior employees, it would not, in all probability, make any happier reading.

To the men at the top, a massive part of their task often seems to lie in force-feeding middle managers with the necessities of marketing and the other basic components of modern management. All too often, the hunger strike continues: the managers won't swallow the diet. True, in the public sector, high, senior, middle and junior management alike suffer from the same disability. They operate in an environment where true competition either doesn't exist at all, or is tremendously diminished in force by the absence of management and marketing's ultimate sanction – the need to make a profit or die.

But the truth which the private sector dare not forget is that it's possible, very possible, to be making excellent profits – while still dying inch by inch as the habits of success strangle the initiatives of innovation at birth. In the Age of Competition what you are doesn't count, still less what you were: the supreme determinant is what the company is going to be.

5: The Full Nelson Necessity

The connection between marketing and the mayhem caused by an unwelcome takeover bid may not be immediately obvious. On the contrary: in the retaliatory wave of counter-attacks and self-defence by the affronted management, their feats of marketing are certain to be hymned to the heavens. And it is, of course, probable that the company's market position is its main attraction to the predator.

Thus Tate & Lyle, Letraset and Berec were respectively UK market leaders in sugar, adhesive lettering, and small batteries when their managers learnt of unwelcome takeover bids – and few discoveries are more likely to put a manager off his feed then learning of such an assault on his beloved company. You could practically hear the intense sigh of relief breathed by the new chief executive at Tate & Lyle when a large multi-national predator, on being told that the management would oppose a takeover, quietly and politely vanished. How deeply the embattled boards of Berec and Letraset must have wished that their predators had done the same – a reprieve rarely granted.

Managers do have this extraordinary knack of deciding that it is against the shareholders' interests to agree to a bid which (by complete coincidence, of course) the above-mentioned managers also detest, and for obvious reasons. Not only will they certainly lose their independence and possibly their jobs, but an unwelcome bid is usually an indictment of some managerial sin of omission or commission. For instance, nobody (even at Letraset) could deny that in buying the stamps of Stanley Gibbons the management committed one of the greatest gaffes in recent business history.

It wasn't just that Letraset overpaid by amounts so ludicrous as to be grotesque. The board had sinned against the golden rule of acquisitions. Unless you're in the acquisition business (like Hanson Trust, the villain of Berec's piece), it is generally folly to venture into any purchase outside the markets you know and love. Letraset had even had a diversification crisis before. In the late 1960s it had taken a woeful crack at the packaging business – and that should have taught its management a more lasting lesson.

In Berec's case, a sin of omission leapt out from a glance at its market capitalization before the Hanson bid – as low as £38 million. How could a company with a marvellous brand name like Ever Ready, operating all over Europe and Africa, get to a point where £1 in the stock market bought £6 of turnover? In 1972, by stark and startling contrast, £1 bought only 75p of sales. Berec used to be one of the 100 largest companies in Britain by market value: its last independent summer's value wasn't even in the top 200.

The strengths of the 1960s, which included that splendid brand name, were not exploited to turn Berec into a far larger and more formidable competitor in electrical markets. Sales growth came: nearly 600 per cent in 1966–80: but for the fatal three years average margins on turnover fell to half those achieved in 1972–3: and that tells its own sad story. Managers passionately dislike hostile bids at times of corporate weakness. But the weakness is seldom an act of God. The sense of injustice which they feel is nothing but self-pity. Nemesis comes to those who neglect their markets.

Whatever Happened to Baby Hoover?

In some cases the neglect is so extreme, so puzzling, and the results so drastic as to raise that doom-laden question, Whatever happened to. . . ? For example, whatever happened to Baby Hoover? This British company, child of an American parent, grew so strong that it became the brightest jewel in the parental crown. In 1960 few companies seemed better poised for rich and lasting success: multinational, Europe-oriented, leader in unsaturated consumer markets with weak domestic opposition, proud possessor of a great household name, famous for productive efficiency, blessed with access to American know-how and market developments through its US ownership. How could it fail?

Yet success didn't come. The closing of Perivale, once the focal point of the whole British appliance industry, was only symbolic of a long and sad two-stage decline. Over the ten years to 1981, on cumulative sales figures of £1,571 million, Hoover earned a total net profit of £54.5 million – a pitiful 3.5 per cent. That followed a desperately dreary decade in the 1960s (1969 sales were only £3 million up on 1959). Thereafter in the early 1970s Hoover did smartly pull up its socks and its sales; but the rot set in again. In 1980 turnover was only 27 per cent up on 1975, while the accompanying five-year plunge in profits had reached vanishing point. By contrast Black and Decker trebled both profits and sales between 1973 and 1979.

Even if you argue that Black and Decker's markets for electrically powered appliances were better ones, who deserves the credit for that? It was an Englishman, Robert Appleby, who built this UK subsidiary of an American parent into an intensively managed model of how to conduct and develop a fast-mover in consumer durables. Another Englishman, Sir Charles Colston, had created Hoover's enormously strong position in Britain and Europe in an earlier era. But where Appleby was rewarded with honours and the Number Two spot at the parent organization, Colston was awarded the boot – kicked out by Herbert Hoover, Jr.

That wouldn't have mattered if, after an affronted US management had putsched Herbie himself in 1967, the UK operation had sustained development either on B&D lines (as a crack, independent subsidiary) or on those of British Ford (as part of a US-controlled, trans-European, locally and strongly co-ordinated organization). Perhaps the critical moment was the 1965 Bashing of Bloom. Did Hoover ever learn the true lesson of John Bloom's brief hour of glory with his awful cut-price washing machines? Bloom, before his crash, proved that he was more in touch with Hoover's market than Hoover itself. As far stronger challengers arrived from places like Italy, it's small wonder that the Princes of Perivale found themselves being bashed in turn by the Borgias of the appliance industry. Machiavelli could have told them what to do. If you hold mastery in the marketplace, you never, never let go.

VW's Double Whopper

The menace lies in the mastery itself. That every success carries within it the seeds of its own potential destruction is a truism: but it's one that

207

managements ignore precisely because they are successful. It explains how one great company let sales of its most important product in its most valuable foreign market halve in a single year. The company was Volkswagen; the beleaguered market was the US: and the product was the Rabbit (the Golf in Europe). The year was 1982, and one reason for the collapse, of course, was the general US recession, courtesy of President Reagan. But the Rabbit run–down also raises two fascinating questions:

1. Had VW kept the Rabbit running too long because it thought it had another Beetle?

2. Had VW's decision to assemble its cars in the US, and to promulgate the fact assiduously, backfired – because, to quote an analyst, 'people were willing to pay more for a foreign car', but . . . 'it became hard to convince consumers that there was something unique about a car made in Pennsylvania'?

On the first point, VW got in the deepest possible trouble with the Beetle itself: notoriously, the latter lived on far, far too long, with the entire company's fortunes pinned to its snub nose, because the management couldn't bring itself to admit that its beloved Beetle was obsolete – or to agree on how to replace it. In today's world market, you can't afford to run a Rabbit (launched 1974) indefinitely: certainly not at a time when a Ford had launched its three leading lower–priced ranges in 1977, 1980, and 1982.

As for that 'made in America' label, the advertising stress was making the best of a bad job. VW felt that US assembly was essential to counteract the then strength of the D-mark. Once the boot was on the dollar's foot the Rabbit, despite price cuts, cost notably more than its Mazda or Toyota rivals. As in its calamitous purchase of Triumph-Adler's business machines, VW simply got its strategy wrong: but this time in its base business and key markets.

The company came back from the edge of the grave famously before. After record-breaking losses, new management pushed through a total revamp of production facilities and model range in a single amazing year, as the Golf ousted the Beetle. But some journeys back are too long ever to be made. Note three vital statistics: 500,000, the American sales of VWs (mostly Beetles) in 1971; 150,000, the sales in 1984: and 560,000 – the US sales figure for Toyota in that same year. Clearly nothing short of a new Beetle, probably not even a new Rabbit, will restore VW to the palmy days of eleven years before. In marketing you can get away with one whopping error, but seldom with two – especially if it's the *same* error.

The Vulnerable Grand Slam

Gigantic companies like VW, though, never face the ultimate sanctions of total collapse or private takeover, simply because they are so gigantic. The worst fate to which they are liable is the kind of lingering life-after-death in which BL passed so many years after its takeover by the state. But that possibility doesn't contain the same threat of imminent execution that so concentrates the mind of lesser managements (or managements of lesser companies).

Unfortunately, the action to which the concentrated mind turns can't address the real cause of vulnerability – the marketing failure. Marketing is essentially a long-term business, on the way up and on the way down. The defensive moves, indeed, often include getting out of markets rather than tightening the company's grip on them. Thus Bowater, in a brave act of bifurcation, setting its North American side adrift, completely reversed the latter, westward-ho direction of founder Sir Eric Bowater's fearsome drive. It takes guts for a great corporation to turn its back so decisively on the past. The decision spoke volumes for the force of the new marketing wisdom: that organization must fit the markets, not the other way round.

The out-dated or over-taken approach, what you might call upside-down marketing, has become impossible to maintain in an era when competition from right-way-up marketers is so intense. Company after company, each according to its needs, is thus reorganizing round core markets, throwing out the rubbish (or, in the accurate words of Dr Ingram Lenton, the Bowater managing director, 'no-hope businesses') to reduce their vulnerability.

Thus, in the ferocious personal computer market, the Apple empire struck back at IBM in 1984 – outselling the brand-new but disappointing PC jr with the older-fangled Apple IIe, and selling out its own brilliant infant Macintosh. Market after market has gone or is going the same way, with a few powerful contenders striving for victory with strategies that are broadly me-too. Every would-be champion is pouring wealth into new facilities and new products, each trying to achieve the thrice-blessed combination of lowest cost, highest added value and top quality.

It follows that a moment's weakness costs dear. IBM slipped in announcing the PC jr three months before it could deliver (what's known in the trade, or should be, as 'doing a Sinclair'): and the product had defects of specification and consumer appeal. Result: rich reprieve for Apple. In the video star wars, the great RCA chose the wrong direction, discs instead of cassettes. Result: losses of $580 million and a $175 million write-off on closure.

Never have great companies had their weaknesses, temporary or permanent, more swiftly and ruthlessly exposed. Thus, the stunning saga of the General Electric Company returned, in a sorry way, to whence it came with the sale of its half-share in British TV manufacture to its partner, Hitachi. The Hirwaun plant in which GEC thus literally lost interest was once the pride and joy of Radio and Allied, the family controlled company which young Arnold Weinstock master-minded into so strong a position that the far from masterful GEC bought it.

The result is history: a tale of efficient drive with not even a parallel among the post-war, mostly lumbering giants of British industry. In 1966, Hirwaun was an all-GEC success story, with much-envied production costs and controls, and not a Japanese (or Japanese TV) in sight. Since then Lord Weinstock's company has multiplied its net income twenty times to £388 million. Sales, moreover, have quadrupled, making it absurd to argue (as many acid critics have done, nevertheless) that the Weinstock achievement has been solely negative, a matter of cutting back, tightening up and screwing down.

The splendid positive achievement inevitably poses a giant conundrum. How could so proven a management, led with such famous effectiveness, end up with no manufacturing position in mainline consumer electronics – industries which are among the stars of the world economic show? How was it, too, that partner Hitachi, to quote the *Financial Times*, 'has been more successful . . . than GEC and has been taking up to 80 per cent of the production from Hirwaun?'.

Part of the explanation is that GEC has concentrated on industrial and defence products rather than consumer goods – the latter being an intensely competitive cockpit where, to tell the sad truth, GEC's powers of mass marketing and innovation have never been very evident. The wisdom of this strategy is laid wide open to doubt, however, by the success of Hitachi (and others) in having the best of both worlds: the Japanese champion had *double* GEC's world sales in 1983.

Moreover, the consumer and industrial technologies, and the marketing of both, are converging. Thus, the arch–industrial AT&T, having barely stuck a nose outside American telecommunications all its life, unveiled, at about the time GEC quit Hirwaun, a strong range of world-targeted compatible computers, aimed at the heart of competitors which include, of course, the mighty marketing machine of IBM. That's another bus which GEC has missed. So have its major European competitors, to be fair: but they too, may live (and probably have lived) to regret it.

The number of major business sectors which any company, however great, can afford to miss in the markets of the eighties is strictly limited. Too many missed businesses, and any company short of gigantism is somebody else's potential purchase (and, given the fates of Thomas Tilling and Gulf Oil, even giants aren't safe), the sovereign importance of establishing a full Nelson hold on its prime market or markets is inescapable. Hold on like grim death, as the best marketing companies do, and at best the company will live happily and profitably ever after. At worst, at least the purchaser, hated or welcomed, will be forced to pay through the nose.

6: Micro-Economic Marketing

That omnipresence of change is a cliché of the eighties. Yet the full significance of what has already happened in the naked world market, let alone what is going to happen, in the period to the nineties and beyond has only started to sink in. The first certainty is that there are no certainties – and anybody who doubts that need only look at the devastation, not of the oil industry, but of the forecasts which predicted oil shortage and price escalation for ever.

What actually happened, the crumbling away in the oil market, is a powerful, and maybe ominous demonstration that the basic law of all markets will never be suspended: what goes up must come down. If what's rising is a price, sooner or later the higher cost will choke off demand, encourage substitution and create a mounting surplus. With equal certainty, that glut will press harder and harder on prices until – hey presto! – it's no longer Yamani or your life.

But the law doesn't only apply to prices. Lovely, soaring profits eventually have the ugly effect of attracting competition: so that even a superb computer company like Digital Equipment finds its market share receding inexorably, to the point where it can no longer take recession in its stride. Instead, it suffers severe decline in profits. If that's painful, merely look at the slaughter that affected weaker firms, as IBM's Personal Computer took its inevitable lion's share of a market where far too many kittens had been making their small fortunes.

Even big Apple, having hired its first-ever marketing supremo, has had to solve some vile problems as it fought back against IBM – managing to sell the make-or-break Lisa and Macintosh marvels, without undermining its vital business with the excellent Apple II.

When a market breaks, as have both Apple's and Sheik Yamani's, those engaged have to remember one thing above all: the process is ineluctable. Once the basic economies of the marketplace have asserted themselves in this way, they can't be overturned.

Hence the truth that you can fix all of the markets some of the time, but none of the markets all of the time. The textbook answer to these dilemmas is that the company should establish so clear a marketing superiority that it is invulnerable – offering the highest perceived value at the highest price. The paradigm of this approach is Caterpillar Tractor. Yet, as noted, it made losses for the first time in its history, because of recession coupled with inability to match the fleetness of foot of Komatsu, its once far tinier Japanese competitor.

The tragedy is that the superior marketer may build so superior a market share, and saturate the market so efficiently, that the company has nowhere to hide when recession strikes. The only course is to recognize that, one day, marketing's law of gravity will affect every business, and that the force bringing the law into play, as likely as not, will be international competition. The global transportation revolution is basic here: but so is the new technology which allows, say, unskilled Asians to assemble and export high-tech products.

To make matters worse, currency movements make it impossible to predict exactly where the most cutting competition will emerge. In early 1982 the joker in the pack was the US, whose currency had fallen so heavily against the Deutschmark that exporting suddenly became fun for American corporations – and much more profitable. That challenge passed, but Japan's won't: with its inefficient domestic economy and total need for imported materials, Japan has no option but to develop still more highly competitive export industries.

Since most Western economies will also be trying to export more (if only to eliminate their energy deficits), you can bank on tough competition for as far as the eye cares to see. So how does the poor marketer manage? Actually, much as he was forced to manage from 1973 onwards.

1. Seeking higher added value first, rather than higher volume, by optimizing prices and reducing costs.

2. Going for specialized world markets rather than domestic commodity ones.

3. Taking his micro-economic opportunities where he finds them.

213

What's In An Industry?

There'll be plenty of opportunities: but they won't be in traditional industry. Indeed, what is industry? That might sound like a silly question, until you consider a fact like this: the fifth or so largest employer in the US isn't in cars, or oil, or steel, or computers. It's in hamburgers – none other than the Big Mac itself.

If industry means converting raw materials into consumable products, McDonald's is as industrious, so to speak, as General Motors. True, the product isn't durable, and the materials consist entirely of food. But food manufacturers count as an industry – so why is a fast food processor a mere service? Anyway, why are 'services' mere? For that matter, how many of the people employed in industry, like marketing men, are rather more remote from actually making things than a short order cook?

The definitions matter for both the economy and the business of management. What's traditionally defined as 'industry' notoriously employs far fewer people than it did – especially at the blunt end. At the sharp end, where the product meets the customer, industry employs more and more, directly and indirectly. The analogy is with agriculture. Numbers actually working on the land have become minute: but great hordes are now occupied in transforming farm produce and delivering the results, often in fantastical guises, to the waiting mouths. Really, the staffs of RHM and Wall's, Eden Vale and McDonald's are part of the agricultural industry.

Agriculture's dwindling away as an employer of labour is an optical illusion. The action has simply moved downstream. True, in some cases (like steel), the action has moved away from a whole industry, for reasons that won't be reversed. In others, like cars, though, the action has moved from blunt-end companies to sharp, market-oriented ones: the extraordinary results of BMW and Mercedes, growing richly yet again while rivals groaned, rest on superbly efficient service of defined market segments. Similarly, Sweden's L.M. Ericsson has an absurdly high world market share in public telephone exchanges, which is a just reward for starting at the sharp end, and setting out deliberately to provide customers with their heart's desire in electronic switching.

The Battles of Britain

Re-industrialization is the real word for what's happening – a redistribution of manpower and resources round a world economy in which market needs are changing fast. Britain's 'de-industrialization', however, is sadly special, because in many industries, declining or rising, British companies, failing to maintain market shares, have probably passed the point of no return. That is as much a threat in so-called services as in *soi-disant* industry. It can't be countered by creating jobs (whatever that means), but only by exploiting markets – and in that task Britain will need far more than the Dunkirk spirit. Unfortunately the economic Dunkirk has been and gone: and this time the troops were left on the beaches. In the war for European business supremacy Britain's manufacturers have been so far behind in key sectors that even the spirit of Japan, let alone Dunkirk, wouldn't enable them to catch up.

Merely glance over the leaders in Europe's markets. In cars, Britain can only play a strictly subordinate part. The star roles have gone irreversibly to US, French, and German companies. In chemicals, ICI has a position much larger than that of any other UK company in any other great industry: yet each of the Big Three German companies is of comparable size.

In the electrical and electronics sectors, all the remarkable progress made by GEC has still left it looking positively under-sized against Siemens or Philips. Go on through the industrial categories – appliances, food, mechanical engineering, etc., etc. – and you will find precious few major businesses where Britain has the leaders in either scale, or share of the key markets, or technology, or proportion of world exports. The chances of mounting, not a Dunkirk (which was, after all, a glorious defeat), but an El Alamein are so remote that even to consider them is wishful thinking of the worst kind.

The Montgomery strategy is, however, the only one that is any use in seeking to achieve major presence in Western Europe or any of the world's intensely competitive markets. You mass your resources at the critical point, achieve clear superiority over the competition, and press home your advantage remorselessly. If the other side commands greater resources by far, though, even a managerial Monty is helpless. So Britain has lost the war – which doesn't mean that every future battle is lost.

The lesson for management is that strategy must cease to be grand. Given its relative lack of resources and scale, the typical British manufacturing company has no real option but to specialize in intelligently selected markets where it can hope to capitalize on the national skills, cashing in on the fact that the retreat from other markets has left micro-capacity of many kinds, from manpower to R&D, which can definitely be exploited to good micro-economic effect.

For the nation, as for individual companies, the lesson is that, in an era when victory was supposed to go to the big battalions, market after market has been scooped by the relatively small. From now to the end of the century, the old, across-the-board markets that made the corporations mighty will no longer hold sway. The emperor is as naked as everybody else in marketing when the specialities are so infinite. And specialism is a game that anybody can play: with one proviso – that they play it especially well.

216

Heller's Golden Rules

HOW TO . . .

. . . AVOID COME-UPPANCE

1: Make realism your ultimate safeground

2: If a business seems to be successfully ignoring the logic of markets, don't believe it

3: Insist first, foremost and last on getting the right results

. . . ACHIEVE SAFETY

1: Realize that a little misfortune can be a big help

2: Aim for the lowest costs in the least locations

3: Learn the lessons of failure and repeat those of success

. . . GAIN GROWTH

1: Be bold in marketing plans – but not foolhardy

2: Take the challenge to the competition, wherever it is

3: Base the plans and the challenge on investment – in products *and* their marketing

. . . KEEP MOVING

1: Get out of the office and talk to the market

2: Never defend the *status quo* simply because it is the *status quo*

3: Get out of the office and talk to your managers

. . . HANG ON

1: Remember that a large market position isn't a strength, but an opportunity – and a threat

2: If you hold mastery in the marketplace, defend it masterfully

3: Bear in mind that one false step is hard, maybe impossible, to retrieve

. . . EXPLOIT THE EIGHTIES

1: Go for higher added value, specialized world markets, and every micro-economic opportunity you can

2: Provide superbly efficient service of defined market segments

3: Mass resources at the critical point, achieve clear superiority and press home your advantage: if you can't, stay away

Index